# BIG ENGLISH 6 PLUS

AF147547

## Contents

**Pearson Education Limited**
Edinburgh Gate
Harlow
Essex CM20 2JE
England
and Associated Companies throughout the world.

www.pearsonelt.com/bigenglish

© Pearson Education Limited 2015

Authorised adaptation from the United States edition entitled Big English,
1st Edition, by Mario Herrera and Christopher Sol Cruz. Published by Pearson
Education Inc. © 2013 by Pearson Education, Inc.

The right of Mario Herrera and Christopher Sol Cruz to be identified as the
authors of this Work have been asserted by them in accordance with the
Copyright, Designs and Patents Act 1988.

First published 2015

ISBN: 978-1-4479-8961-5

Set in Apex Sans

**Acknowledgements**

The publisher would like to thank the following for their kind permission to
reproduce their photographs:

(Key: b-bottom; c-centre; l-left; r-right; t-top)

**123RF.com:** Tono Balaguer 85b; **Alamy Images:** Ace Stock Limited 37, Allstar
Picture Library 120l, Anders Blomqvist 139b, Sabena Jane Blackbird 92tl, Blend
Images 48c/5, 76tc, blickwinkel 92tr, Design Pics Inc 4tr, 6bl, 13tr, dieKleinert
105, 134tr, Ilya Genkin 106cl, geogphotos 70t, GL Archive 24, Glow Asia RF 5br,
48cr/5, Hemis 92cl, 134tc, i love images 23, Image Source 18tc, Image Source
Plus 121c, INTERFOTO 126, Jamie Pham Photography 121l, JHPhoto 127, Eddie
Linssen 76tr, MBI 32c, Megapress 48r/5, michel platini FERNANDES BORGES
17, Jeff Morgan 14 133, 134bl, OJO Images Ltd 32cl, 125, rgbstudio 18tr, Marc
Romanelli 114l, Chris Rout 32tr, RubberBall 40tr, 138, SuperStock / RGB
Ventures 25; **Corbis**: Juice Images / Ian Lishman 4cl, KidStock / Blend Images
32cr, Ocean 4tc, Reuters / David Bebber 130, Wavebreak Media Ltd /Alloy 10,
ZenShui / Sigrid Olsson 49tr; **Datacraft Co Ltd:** 76c; **Digital Vision:** 110; **DK
Images:** Angela Coppola 4cr, Linda Whitwam 142; **Fotolia.com:** Goran Bogicevic
76tl, bst2012 40br, CandyBox Images 49c, chawalitpix 68, Eléonore H 19, 49cr,
faizzaki 82, feferoni 93b, 101r, fergregory 48tr, gavran333 40tl, godfer 34,
grafikplusfoto 26l, hansenn 114r, Iva 106tr, J_Foto 33l, 49tl, Kara-Kotsya 76cl,
KaYann 106tl, 111, koya979 48tc, Kzenon 120r, michaeljung 36, Felix
Mizioznikov 32tl, napgalleria 48tl, PiLensPhoto 93t, 101l, 134tl, pumpchn 13l,
Andres Rodriguez 53, 56l, Sabphoto 18cr, 26r, Subbotina Anna 107tl, 116,
134cr, S. White 48l/5; **Getty Images:** Blend Images / Ariel Skelley 4c, Mark
Bowden 31tc, 32tc, 45, André De Kesel 77c, Fuse 4tl, 76cr, 85tr, Gallo Images /
Danita Delimont 108, Sheldon Levis 56r, SCIEPRO / Science Photo Library 54b;
**Glow Images:** Perspectives 18tl; **Pearson Education Ltd:** 92c, 94, 137, Gareth
Boden 13b; **PhotoDisc:** Ryan McVay 18cl; **Rex Features:** View Pictures 56c;
**Shutterstock.com:** AVAVA 31, 129t, Galina Barskaya 6cl, Blend Images 66bl,
Ross Brown 28, CandyBox Images 9, 15, chungking 106cr, Costazzurra 48cl,
Creatista 66br, Robert Crum 33r, 139t, Dim Dimich 20, edg 121r, 134br, 144,
erashov 129b, Tara Flake 5tl, Giuseppe_R 66tl, Dieter Hawlan 86b, holbox 40bl,
Hubis 54t, Matthew Jacques 106tc, JaySi 70b, jsouthby 129bc, Kamira 86t,
karelnoppe 58, kouptsova 5bl, R. Gino Santa Maria 5tr, milias1987 39, Monkey
Business Images 27r, 85tl, 97, Nella 107c, Nestor Noci 107tr, 134c, Odua
Images 52r, Oleg_Mit 52l, Anna Omelchenko 124, 134bc, Pete Pahham 27l,
Edyta Pawlowska 46, photogl 18c, Stuart G Porter 77t, Phon Promwisate 107tc,
134cl, Ivaschenko Roman 112, Julian Rovagnati 6tl, S-F 70cr, silver-john 141,
Slazdi 107cr, Somchai Som 107cl, 143, szefei 61, Aleksandar Todorovic 106c,
Kiselev Andrey Valerevich 12, Tracy Whiteside 66tr, Ann Worthy 129tc, Lisa F.
Young 100; **SuperStock:** age fotostock 14, Fine Art Images 77b, 89

**Cover images:** Front: **Corbis:** Tetra Images / Rob Lewine r; **Shutterstock.com:**
Kamira l, Pi-Lens c

All other images © Pearson Education

Every effort has been made to trace the copyright holders and we apologise in
advance for any unintentional omissions. We would be pleased to insert the
appropriate acknowledgement in any subsequent edition of this publication.

**Illustrated by**

Zaharias Papadopoulos (Hyphen), Q2A Media Services, Anthony Lewis, Christos
Skaltsas (Hyphen).

# Big English Song

From the mountaintops to the bottom of the sea,
From a big blue whale to a baby bumblebee-
If you're big, if you're small, you can have it all,
And you can be anything you want to be!

**It's bigger than you. It's bigger than me.**
**There's so much to do and there's so much to see!**
**The world is big and beautiful and so are we!**
**Think big! Dream big! Big English!**

So in every land, from the desert to the sea
We can all join hands and be one big family.
If we love, if we care, we can go anywhere!
The world belongs to everyone; it's ours to share.

**It's bigger than you. It's bigger than me.**
**There's so much to do and there's so much to see!**
**The world is big and beautiful and so are we!**
**Think big! Dream big! Big English!**

**It's bigger than you. It's bigger than me.**
**There's so much to do and there's so much to see!**
**The world is big and beautiful and waiting for me.**
**A One, two, three...**
**Think big! Dream big! Big English!**

# ALL ABOUT SCHOOL

**1** What school activities do you see in the pictures? Write the numbers.

___ going on a field trip

___ working on computers

___ doing a project

___ giving a presentation

___ taking a test

___ practicing yoga

**2** Read and ✓. What would you like your school to have?

| | lots of | some | none |
|---|:---:|:---:|:---:|
| **1** free time | ☐ | ☐ | ☐ |
| **2** homework | ☐ | ☐ | ☐ |
| **3** tests | ☐ | ☐ | ☐ |
| **4** group projects | ☐ | ☐ | ☐ |
| **5** after-school clubs | ☐ | ☐ | ☐ |
| **6** independent work | ☐ | ☐ | ☐ |
| **7** field trips | ☐ | ☐ | ☐ |
| **8** computers | ☐ | ☐ | ☐ |

 **3** Check (✔) the verbs you use with each phrase. Then listen and check your answers.

| | | do | study for | hand in | finish | take |
|---|---|---|---|---|---|---|
| **1** | a test | | | | | |
| **2** | an essay | | | | | |
| **3** | a book review | | | | | |
| **4** | homework | | | | | |
| **5** | a project | | | | | |

 **4** Read. What should each student have done? Match the name with the advice. Write the letter.

I finished my essay but my puppy ate it when I wasn't looking.

**Katherine**

I left my book on the bus yesterday. I can't hand in my book report.

**Mark**

I didn't start my history project until yesterday. I couldn't finish it last night.

**Tabitha**

I wanted to study for the math test but I started playing video games. And then it was too late. My mom told me to go to bed.

**Dean**

___ **1** Katherine
___ **2** Mark
___ **3** Tabitha
___ **4** Dean

**a** should have paid attention to the time.
**b** should have done it again.
**c** should have done it earlier.
**d** should have been more careful.

**THINK BIG**

Complete the sentences with an excuse or some advice.

**1 A:** Ben hasn't finished his science project because he didn't start it until last night.

**B:** He _____.

**2 A:** Rich _____.

**B:** He should have been more careful.

**5** Listen and read. Circle **T** for true or **F** for false.

ninja_fly

Hi, everyone! What's going on? I need your advice. I have this problem with my mom. My mom has volunteered for every dance, every field trip, and every fundraising activity we've had at school so far this year. Sometimes I like it. But you know something? The kids make fun of me because she's always here. It's embarrassing. I know she thinks the school needs her help but I need her help, too… to stay away. What should I do?

free_mind09

OK, ninja_fly. I understand you. It can be really annoying to have your mom at school all the time. You should tell her how you feel. Ask her to stop volunteering for everything and stop coming to school so often. Take my advice. I had the same problem with my mom and it worked for me.

2good_for_u

I agree with free_mind09. You should tell your mom that it bothers you when she comes to school so often. But I don't think she should stop volunteering. I'll bet she likes it and the school needs it. You should be glad she wants to help. You should tell her that she's a great mom but that you would like her to volunteer at school less often. Think positively!

1 Ninja_fly's mom volunteers too much at his school.      T    F

2 Both free_mind09 and 2good_for_u think ninja_fly      T    F
should tell his mom to stop volunteering so much.

3 Free_mind09 didn't have the same problem with her mom.      T    F

4 2good_for_u thinks volunteering is good.      T    F

**6** Answer the question.

If your mom volunteered at your school, would you feel the same way as ninja_fly? Why/Why not?

_____

_____

**7** Listen and read. Circle the correct answers.

**Jim:** Hi, Ollie. Have you met the new exchange student yet?

**Ollie:** No. Why?

**Jim:** She's from Finland and she's really nice!

**Ollie:** Nice, <u>huh</u>? Is she smart, too?

**Jim:** Very smart. I've talked to her.

**Ollie:** In English?

**Jim:** Of course in English. But maybe I'll start learning Finnish now.

**Ollie:** <u>You're crazy</u>. You haven't even learned English yet and you *are* English.

**Jim:** Finnish is different. I'm sure I'll learn it fast. I'm motivated!

**Ollie:** <u>Yeah, yeah, yeah</u>.

1 Ollie **has seen / hasn't seen** the exchange student.

2 Jim **has already talked / hasn't talked** to the exchange student.

3 The exchange student **speaks / doesn't speak** English.

4 Jim **wants / doesn't want** to speak Finnish to the exchange student.

**8** Look at 7. Circle the correct answers.

1 When Ollie says "Nice, huh?", "huh" means that he's:

   **a** not interested.       **b** interested.

2 "You're crazy" means:

   **a** what you're saying doesn't make any sense.    **b** what you're saying makes sense.

3 The expression "yeah, yeah, yeah" means:

   **a** I like what you say.    **b** I don't believe that you'll do what you say.

**9** Complete the dialogs. Circle the correct expressions. Then listen and check your answers.

1 **A:** I'm going to stop playing video games forever!

   **B:** **Huh? / You're crazy!** You've played video games ever since I met you.

2 **A:** Jeffrey hasn't asked anyone to the dance yet.

   **B:** He hasn't, **yeah, yeah, yeah. / huh?** I wonder who he'll ask.

3 **A:** This time I'm going to hand in my project on time.

   **B:** **You're crazy. / Yeah, yeah, yeah.** That's what you always say but you're always late.

| Has she done her solo yet? | Yes, she has. She has already done it. |
| | No, she hasn't. She hasn't done it yet. |
| Have they ever won an award? | Yes, they have./No, they haven't. |

**10** Read about Mike and Tom. Then write the answers or questions.

## Mike and Tom's Social Science Project

 **8:45 PM** Mike and Tom are playing video games. They haven't started their social science project.

 **2:00 AM** Mike has finished making the model pyramid but Tom hasn't finished his research yet.

 **8:15 AM** Mike and Tom have finished their project. Tom has fallen asleep.

**1** It's 8:45 p.m. Have Mike and Tom gotten supplies for their project yet?

_____

**2** It's 8:45 p.m. Has Mike completed the model of the pyramid yet?

_____

**3** It's 2:00 a.m. Has Tom started doing research on the computer yet?

_____

**4** It's 2:00 a.m. Have Mike and Tom finished their project yet?

_____

**5** It's 8:15 a.m. _____

Yes, they have. Mike and Tom have already arrived in the class.

**6** It's 8:30 a.m. _____

Yes, they have. Mike and Tom have handed in their project.

| | |
|---|---|
| He **has** <u>already</u> **finished** the project. | He **finished** it <u>yesterday</u>. |
| He **hasn't finished** the project <u>yet</u>. | He **didn't finish** it <u>yesterday</u>. |

**11** Look at Sarah's to-do list. Then complete the sentences.

**1** Sarah _____ posters for the art exhibition at 4:00.

**2** She _____ already _____ posters for the art exhibition.

**3** Sarah _____ her book review at 5:30.

**4** She _____ already _____ her book review.

**5** Sarah _____ her science project yet.

**6** Sarah _____ her science project tonight.

> **Things to do:**
>
> 1 Make posters for art exhibition at 4:00 ☑
>
> 2 Start book review at 5:30 ☑
>
> 3 Finish science project tonight ☐

**12** Complete the dialogs. Use the correct form of the verbs in parentheses.

**1** (go)

**A:** Has Kathy _____ to her dance lesson yet?

**B:** Yes, she _____ to her dance lesson at 3:00.

**2** (meet)

**A:** Has Mark _____ the exchange student yet?

**B:** No, he _____ the exchange student yet.

**3** (hand in)

**A:** Has Trudy _____ her homework yet?

**B:** No, she _____ her homework yet.

**4** (eat)

**A:** Has Sean _____ dinner yet?

**B:** Yes, he _____ dinner at 6:00.

**13** Complete the sentences. Circle the correct form of the verbs.

**1** I **have finished / finished** my essay last night but I **haven't handed / didn't hand** it in yet.

**2** Jan **has already taken / took** the test yesterday but she **has studied / didn't study** for it. She should have studied more.

**3** We **haven't started / didn't start** our project yet. We **haven't had / didn't have** time yesterday.

**14** Read the definition. Circle the correct word.

| | | |
|---|---|---|
| **1** | The usual level or amount for most people or things. | **average / schedule** |
| **2** | A formal event in which there is a traditional set of actions or words. | **gather / ceremony** |
| **3** | To come together in the same place. | **packed / gather** |
| **4** | Usual or normal. | **typical / bright** |
| **5** | Not very great or not very much. | **limited / strengthen** |
| **6** | The idea that something is true or right. | **ceremony / belief** |

**15** Listen and read. How long is the typical school day in Poland?

## School in Poland

How long is a typical school day for you? What time do you start and what time do you finish? Most students spend an average of five to six hours at school every day. But in some countries, students spend more time at school and have a packed schedule with many lessons. In other countries, they spend less time at school. Also, students in some countries may study subjects that are different from the ones you have. Do you have classes in each subject every day or do you have some subjects just a few times a week? Most students do math daily, but they may only do art or music two or three times a week. What about tests? How often do you get tested at your school? In some countries, students are tested often. In others, testing is limited. And in some countries, students aren't tested at all!

If you like tests, you wouldn't like going to primary school in Poland! Students in Poland only take one official test, at the end of 6th grade, and they don't get grades for the first three years of school. Would you like that? That doesn't mean that students don't learn. Their schedule includes many subjects to keep them busy. In Poland, students must study the following subjects: art, modern foreign languages (such as German or English), P.E., music, history, civics, science, math, technology, and computer science. They have a lot of these lessons every day to strengthen their skills. Also, each week students take part in various after-school activities, such as sports, theater, or computer clubs. Does your school have any interesting after-school clubs? What after-school clubs have you joined?

The school day is shorter in Poland, too. A typical day starts at 8:00 a.m. and finishes at 12:00 p.m. or 1:00 p.m. That gives students in Poland more free time than in Spain or the UK, for instance. But they don't complain about that! Would you?

**16** Read 15 again and write the answers to the questions.

1 How long is an average school day for most students? _____

2 Which subject do most students study every day? _____

3 When do Polish students take their first official test? _____

4 What languages do Polish students study? _____

5 When do students in Poland do sports, theater, or computer clubs? _____

6 When does a typical school day finish in Poland? _____

**17** Complete the sentences with the words in the box.

daily    free time    tests    schedule    typical

1 Most Polish students are happy with a shorter school day and more _____.

2 In Poland, students study some subjects _____ and others just two or three times a week.

3 A _____ school day in Poland is four or five hours long.

4 A school _____ in Poland includes computer science and civics.

5 Polish students do not take many _____ in primary school.

THINK
BIG

**How does school in Poland compare with your school?**

Write one sentence about how it's different.

_____

_____

Write one sentence about how it's similar.

_____

_____

# Grammar

**18** Read and circle.

1 I **have** / **has** eaten all my lunch.

2 She **haven't** / **hasn't** lived in Turkey for very long.

3 **Have** / **Has** Tomas gone to Greece?

4 **Haven't** / **Hasn't** you finished your homework yet?

5 He has **never** / **ever** played volleyball, because they don't play it at his school.

6 We have studied the Romans **yet** / **already**.

**19** Read and match. Write the letters.

___ **1** Have you ever fallen asleep in class?

___ **2** Has she never heard of that kind of music?

___ **3** Have we finished learning about the Andes?

___ **4** Has he sent the e-mail yet?

___ **5** Have they ever gone abroad?

**a** Yes, we have.

**b** No, they haven't.

**c** No, she hasn't.

**d** Yes, I have.

**e** Yes, he has.

**20** Complete the sentences with the words in the box.

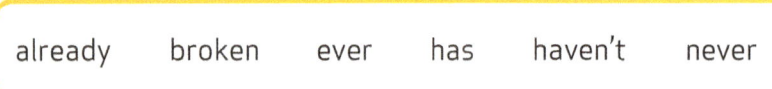

| already | broken | ever | has | haven't | never |

1 Has he _____ your best teapot?

2 We have _____ met our great aunt, because she lives in Canada.

3 Haven't you watched that film three times _____ ?

4 Leyla _____ forgotten her homework at school again!

5 They _____ studied American history yet.

6 Has she _____ thanked you for that beautiful wedding gift?

**21** Unscramble and write the sentences.

1 has worked / on the computer / he / for an hour

_____

2 the drama club / yet / haven't joined / they

_____

3 ever / listened to / have you / the singer, Adele

_____

4 drunk / her milk / already / hasn't she

_____

5 our cousins / twice this year / we've / already / visited

_____

**22** Write answers for you. Use have/haven't or has/hasn't.

1 Have you ever been to a music concert? _____.

2 Has your class ever had a pet? _____.

3 Has your father ever been to China? _____.

4 Have you eaten your supper yet? _____.

**23** Write four questions you could ask a friend. Use Have or Has.

1 _____

2 _____

3 _____

4 _____

**24** Read and match. Write the letters.

___ **1** pace

___ **2** practical

___ **3** memorize

___ **4** curriculum

___ **5** hobby

___ **6** structured

**a** to learn something and to remember it perfectly

**b** an activity you enjoy doing in your free time

**c** the way something is organized

**d** a way to describe something real, not just an idea

**e** all the subjects that students learn at school

**f** the speed at which something happens

**25** Listen and read. Then complete the chart.

# Differences in Education

All around the world, children go to school. Yet, education in one country may be very different than education in another country. Schools may differ in the number of hours that students spend there every day. They may also be different in the subjects that students can study, or the pace with which they move through the curriculum. They may differ in the number of tests that students have to take, too, as well as how often they have to take these tests.

Education in Finland, China, and Poland is different in some ways, but students in all these countries do well on achievement tests. Finland has the highest scores in science, math, and reading, yet students go to school for only four hours a day, on average. That's quite amazing! Most students in Poland are at school a little longer. In China, children are in school from 8 to 11 hours a day.

Class size is also different. In Finland, classes are small. The average class size is 18. Classes in Poland have about 25 students. In China, they're much larger. The way the school day is structured is different, too. Students in China and Poland follow schedules, but in Finland, students decide what they want to do each day. The teacher gives them practical choices and the students decide.

Students in these countries don't do a lot of homework. Is homework important? People have very different opinions on this topic. The interesting thing is that students in these countries learn a lot without doing a lot of homework or memorizing facts. They have more time to enjoy learning about things outside the classroom, or to do hobbies. Do you think that's the reason their test scores are so high?

| | Finland | China | Poland |
| --- | --- | --- | --- |
| How many hours of school? | 4 | 1 _____ | 4–5 |
| How large are classes? | 2 _____ | 37 | 3 _____ |
| Is there a schedule? | 4 _____ | 5 _____ | Yes |
| How much time do students spend doing homework each day? | Half an hour daily | One hour daily | One hour daily |

**26** Read **25** again and circle **T** for true or **F** for false.

1 Students in Finland do well on achievement tests. **T    F**

2 Children in China spend more time at school than children in Poland. **T    F**

3 Class size is the largest in Poland. **T    F**

4 Students in Finland have a strict school schedule. **T    F**

5 Children in Finland do more homework than children in China. **T    F**

**27** Find and circle the six words from **24**.

| c | u | r | r | i | c | u | l | u | m |
|---|---|---|---|---|---|---|---|---|---|
| v | t | l | b | v | r | e | w | i | e |
| p | r | a | c | t | i | c | a | l | m |
| a | n | l | c | t | e | i | s | p | o |
| c | o | e | h | o | b | b | y | l | r |
| e | r | w | f | m | k | k | t | j | i |
| b | w | r | u | i | m | u | y | t | z |
| z | n | b | b | p | w | h | n | a | e |
| s | t | r | u | c | t | u | r | e | d |

If you could choose subjects to study, which would you choose? Why?

THINK BIG

_____

_____

In an opinion paragraph, you share your opinion about a topic. To write an opinion paragraph, follow these steps:

- Write your opinion. Use your opinion as the title of your opinion paragraph. For example:

  *Longer School Days Will Not Improve Grades*

- To begin your opinion paragraph, rewrite the title of your paragraph as a question. Then answer the question with your opinion:

  *Will longer school days improve grades? In my opinion, they won't.*

- Next, write reasons for your opinion:

  *Students will be too tired after a longer school day to do their homework. They'll have less time to work on school projects and study for tests.*

- Then, write suggestions:

  *I think offering after-school study periods for students who need extra help is a better idea. Teachers could also organize more group projects. That way, students could help each other while they complete assignments.*

- Finally, write a conclusion:

  *In my opinion, offering extra help to students and organizing more group projects are better ideas than having longer school days. Longer school days might even cause students to get even lower grades because they'll be tired and more stressed.*

**28** Choose one of the school issues below.

- Students **should / shouldn't** use cell phones at school.

- It's **important / not important** to use computers in the classroom.

State your opinion here: _____

**29** Write an outline for your topic in 28. Complete the chart below.

| Title rewritten as question: |
| --- |
| Main opinion: |
| Reason: |
| Suggestion: |
| Conclusion: |

**30** Write an opinion paragraph on a separate piece of paper. Use your information from 29.

**31** Read. Unscramble the questions. Use the present perfect form of the verbs. Then complete the answers.

DONE
Do my social science homework

Finish my science project

**Anna**

NOT DONE
Study for math test

**1** yet / Anna / do / social science homework

Q: _____

A: _____

**2** study for / math test / her / she / yet

Q: _____

A: _____

**3** she / finish / yet / science project / her

Q: _____

A: _____

**32** Complete the sentences. Use the correct form of the verbs in parentheses.

**1** Mark _____ (study) for his math test yesterday.

**2** Sarah _____ (finish) her book report last week.

**3** John _____ (hand in, not) his history assignment yet.

**4** Marissa _____ already _____ (do) her homework.

**33** Write the answer.

George didn't hand in his essay because he fell asleep and didn't finish it. What should he have done? Choose the best idea in the box. Add an idea of your own.

done it earlier    done it again    paid less attention to the time

_____

_____

# unit 2 AMAZING YOUNG PEOPLE

**1** Match the pictures with the sentences about life dreams. Write the numbers.

Someday I would like to...

- [ ] create a photography blog
- [ ] be a professional soccer player
- [ ] climb a mountain
- [ ] start my own band
- [ ] volunteer in Africa
- [ ] find a cure for diseases

**2** Write down four of your dreams. Rank them by importance. 1 = most important. 4 = least important.

1 _____   2 _____

3 _____   4 _____

**3** Look at 2. Which of your dreams will be the most difficult to achieve? Draw a box around it. Which dream will be the easiest to achieve? Underline it. Which dream can you achieve right now? Write it here:

_____

**4** Read. Then circle **T** for true or **F** for false.

My parents are amazing people! My mom's a writer. She wrote and published her first book when she was just 14 years old! She also speaks three languages: English, Spanish, and French. My dad is a famous chess player. He has played chess for over 20 years and has won many tournaments. He also plays the piano and the guitar. My parents are amazing people for all their achievements– especially for being wonderful parents to me and my sister!

Our children are amazing! Our son Chris is great at science. At just ten years old, he started his own science club. The club meets every Friday after school. Last week, he won an award for his latest invention: a portable mp3 case that protects your mp3 player from getting wet! He wants to be a doctor when he grows up. Emma's a terrific athlete! She's the captain of her track and soccer teams. Her soccer team has just won a big soccer tournament. Emma won the Most Valuable Player award! Emma loves being active… her biggest dream is to climb a mountain one day. We are very proud of our amazing children.

**1** Chris's dad has published a book.          T     F

**2** His mom speaks three languages.          T     F

**3** Chris's dad plays two instruments.          T     F

**4** Chris hasn't invented anything yet.          T     F

**5** Emma's team has just won a soccer tournament.          T     F

**6** Emma has already climbed a mountain.          T     F

**5** Complete the sentences. Use the words in the box.

> invented something     published a book     speak 23 languages     was a contestant

**1** Harry, a young boy from Hampshire, UK, _____ on a TV program called *Junior Bake Off*. He won with his amazing carrot cake.

**2** Kevin Doe _____ amazing when he was only 13. He made batteries from junk and helped bring electricity to people's homes in Sierra Leone.

**3** Timothy Donor taught himself to _____ by the time he was 16.

**4** Adora Svitak _____ about how to write when she was only seven.

THINK **BIG** Which of the achievements in **5** do you think is the most important? Why?

**6** Listen and read. Then answer the questions.

# Adora Svitak

**by Tracy Dorington**

Adora Svitak considers herself a writer, a teacher, and an activist. She began writing when she was four years old. She wrote *Flying Fingers* at age seven. In it, she talks about how important writing is and explains how to write. In 2008, Adora published a book of poetry that she co-wrote with her sister.

Adora says that when she hears children say that reading and writing aren't very important in their lives, she gets upset. She thinks that reading and writing about ideas can help change the world. In 2010, Adora gave a presentation titled *What Adults Can Learn from Kids*. She said that adults need to think like children because children think optimistically and creatively when solving problems. She mentioned children like Ruby Bridges, who helped end segregation in the United States. Adults, on the other hand, think about limitations and problems.

Adora continues to publish her work and give speeches. In 2011, she published her first full-length novel, *Yang in Disguise*. In 2012, Adora won an award given by the National Press Club. At the awards ceremony, she gave a speech about the importance of girls achieving their goals and living their dreams. One of Adora's goals is to win a Nobel Prize.

Adora believes that the way to change the world is to trust children and expect that they'll do great things at a young age. Parents and teachers, she says, have low expectations of students. They don't expect children to achieve much. They expect children to listen and not show their brilliance. This thinking has to change. She says that adults should expect wonderful things and learn to listen to children. The future depends on it.

**1** What's one of Adora's accomplishments?

_____

**2** What's one of Adora's future goals?

_____

**3** How does Adora believe the world should change?

_____

**4** Do you agree or disagree with Adora? Explain your answer.

_____

**7** Listen. Circle **T** for true or **F** for false.

**Jen:** Phil, what's your brother doing on his computer? I can see he's really <u>getting into it</u>.

**Phil:** He's probably working on one of his computer programs.

**Jen:** He writes computer programs? But he's only 12!

**Phil:** I know. He started writing programs when he was about nine.

**Jen:** Nine? That's incredible.

**Phil:** He's in trouble with my parents, though. He wants to <u>drop out</u> of school and work on his programs all day.

**Jen:** <u>You're joking</u>, aren't you?

**Phil:** Yeah, I'm <u>just kidding</u>.

| | | | |
|---|---|---|---|
| **1** | Phil's brother likes computers a lot. | T | F |
| **2** | His brother started working with computers when he was in his teens. | T | F |
| **3** | His parents don't want their children to spend all day on the computer. | T | F |
| **4** | Phil's brother is going to stop going to school. | T | F |

**8** Look at **7**. Read the underlined expressions. Match the expressions with their meanings. Write the letter.

___ **1** get into      **a** say something funny to make people laugh

___ **2** drop out      **b** say something surprising that doesn't sound possible

___ **3** be joking      **c** stop going before you finish

___ **4** be kidding      **d** become interested in

**9** Answer the questions.

**1** Have you ever dropped out of anything? What was it? Why did you drop out?

_____

**2** Are you getting into something interesting this year? What is it? Why do you like it?

_____

**3** Look at **7**. Why did Jen say, "You're joking"?

_____

> How long **has** she **played** the piano?
> She**'s played** the piano <u>for</u> five years.
>
> How long **have** they **known** about William Kamkwamba?
> They**'ve known** about him <u>since</u> they saw a film about him.

**10** Look and draw lines to match the phrases to since or for.

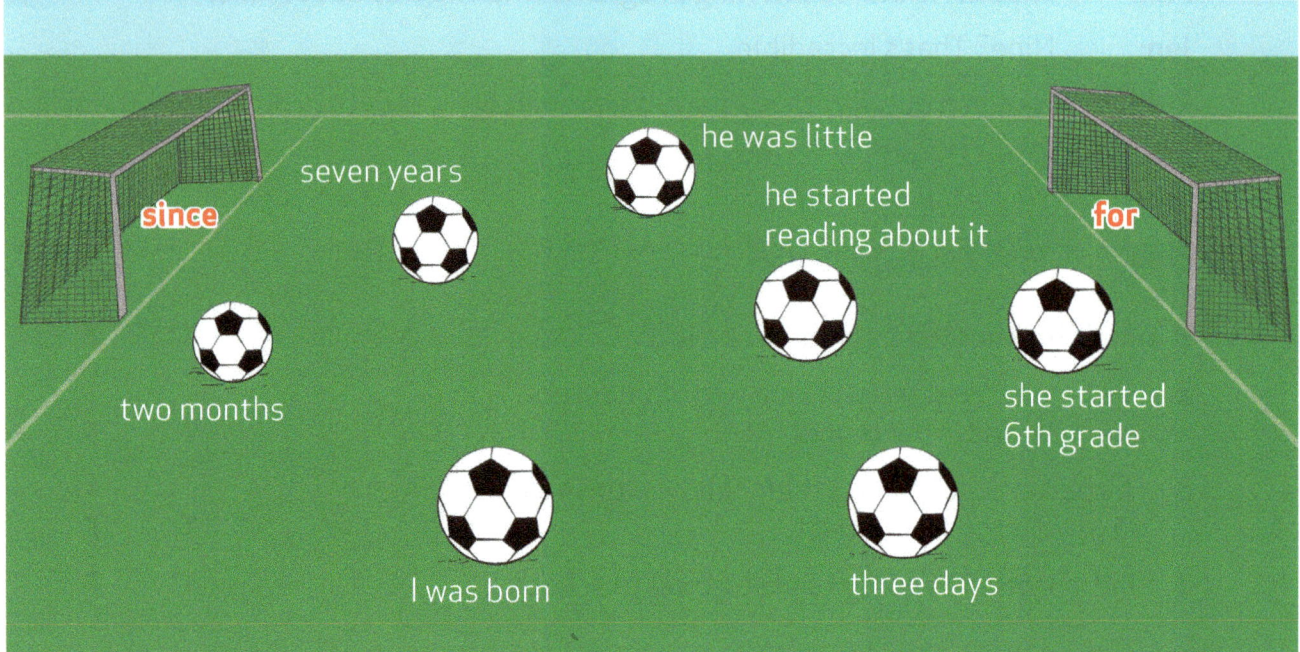

**11** Complete the sentences with the present perfect form of the verbs and for or since.

1 Karen loves swimming. She _____ (swim) competitively _____ she was five.

2 Ray loves reading. He _____ (become) very interested in the Middle Ages _____ he read about it in social science.

3 Francis is taking part in a TV game show. He _____ (study) hard _____ three days.

4 Chloe loves animals. She _____ (volunteer) at the animal shelter _____ two months.

How long **has** your brother **been playing** tennis?
He**'s been playing** tennis <u>since</u> he was five.

How long **have** you and your sister **been bungee jumping**?
We**'ve been bungee jumping** <u>for</u> two years.

**12** Read. Answer the questions. Use the present perfect continuous and the words in parentheses.

Twelve-year-olds Bob and Jenny have their own business, called "Kids Biz." They started working when they were nine. They do jobs like cutting the grass and washing cars. Six months ago, Jenny started babysitting, too. They also volunteer in the community. Bob started collecting money for the animal shelter two years ago. He does that every year. Jenny collects food for the homeless. She started doing that when she was 11. They both blog, too. They started blogging when they started 6th grade.

**1** How long have Bob and Jenny been working?

_____ (since)

**2** How long has Jenny been babysitting?

_____ (for)

**3** How long has Bob been volunteering for the animal shelter?

_____ (for)

**4** How long has Jenny been collecting food for the homeless?

_____ (since)

**5** How long have they been blogging?

_____ (since)

**13** Answer the questions using complete sentences.

**1** Think about something you're studying at school. How long have you been studying it?

_____

**2** Think about something you love doing. How long have you been doing it?

_____

**14** Match the words with the definitions. Write the letters.

___ **1** gifted

___ **2** compose

___ **3** exceptional

___ **4** symphony

___ **5** legend

___ **6** inspiration

**a** a long piece of music written for an orchestra

**b** unusually good

**c** someone famous or admired

**d** having a natural ability to do something very well

**e** something that gives you a great idea

**f** to write a piece of music, poem, speech, etc.

**15** Read and complete with the words from 14. Then listen and check.

# Gifted Children

Many children are talented, but some have ¹_____ abilities that make them famous throughout history. Here are just a few examples of ²_____ children who achieved amazing accomplishments when they were still young:

Wolfgang Amadeus Mozart ³_____ a ⁴_____ at eight and an opera at fourteen – all by himself!

At two years old, Aelita Andre created beautiful paintings that art critics through the ages will admire.

Fourteen-year-old Nadia Comaneci scored a perfect 10 in gymnastics at the Olympic Games—an amazing accomplishment for such a young athlete. As a result, she has become a ⁵_____ in the world of gymnastics!

Another talented child, twelve-year-old Louis Braille from France, changed the world of reading and writing forever when he invented the Braille code to help the blind read and write.

Mozart, Andre, Comaneci and Braille are an ⁶_____ for many people to try to achieve great things!

**16** Read 15 again and circle the correct word.

**1** Mozart composed **a symphony / an opera** when he was fourteen.

**2** When she was **two / twelve**, Aelita Andre created beautiful paintings.

**3** Nadia Comaneci scored a perfect 10 in **diving / gymnastics.**

**4** The twelve-year-old Louis Braille came from **Portugal / France.**

**17** Unscramble the words and write the letters in the boxes. Look at the text in **15** to help you. There's a message for you. Use the numbers and letters to find the message.

MAMPENHICCTLOS
☐☐☐☐☐☐☐☐☐☐☐☐☐☐
5   4   12   13

GASE
☐☐☐☐
8 2

PAEOR
☐☐☐☐☐
10   3

SYNYPHOM
☐☐☐☐☐☐☐☐
9   7

LARLIBE
☐☐☐☐☐☐☐
1 11   6   14

MESSAGE:
☐☐ ☐☐☐☐☐☐ ☐☐☐☐☐☐
1 2   3 4 5   6 7 8   9 10   11 12 13 14

Braille chart:
A B C D E F G H I J
K L M N O P Q R S T
U V W X Y Z
# 1 2 3 4 5 6 7 8 9 0   # 2001

THINK BIG

Mozart composed symphonies and operas because he loved creating music. What do you like creating?

_____

_____

Nadia Comaneci practiced gymnastics every day and was proud of herself and her accomplishments. What accomplishments are you proud of?

_____

_____

Louis Braille is an inspiration because he was blind when he invented Braille to help other blind people read and write. Who or what inspires you?

_____

_____

# Grammar

**18** Read and circle.

1 I **have tried / tried** sushi before, but I don't like it.

2 She **did / has done** her homework yesterday.

3 He **swam / has swum** in competitions since he was nine, so he is a good competitor.

4 On Saturday, we **watched / have watched** the film about that amazing teenager.

5 My cousin **worked / has worked** in Spain since 2013.

6 She **have washed / washed** her hair this morning.

**19** Read and match. Write the letters.

____ 1 Have you ever ridden a camel?

____ 2 Has she ever climbed a mountain?

____ 3 Did he take a lot of photographs?

____ 4 Did she take a shower?

a No, she didn't.

b Yes, he did.

c No, I haven't.

d Yes she has.

**20** Complete the sentences with the correct form of the verbs in parentheses.

1 We _____ (see) many different wild animals when we were on vacation in Africa.

2 He _____ (ride) a horse since he was very young.

3 You _____ (buy) a beautiful gift for your grandmother last year.

4 She _____ (travel) all over South America for the past three years.

5 They _____ (go) to Nepal on a hiking expedition last summer.

**21** Unscramble and write the sentences.

1 worked / his / all day / laptop / he / on

_____

2 concert / the piano / a / in / played / on Friday / she

_____

3 never / to / we've / Costa Rica / been

_____

4 haven't / they / mountain / a / yet / climbed

_____

_____

5 movie / he's / this / seen / already

_____

_____

**22** Write questions for the answers. Use Have / Has...? or Did...?

1 _____ Yes, we have.

2 _____ No, she didn't.

3 _____ Yes, I did.

4 _____ No, he hasn't.

**23** Answer the questions for you.

1 Have you ever been to New York? _____

2 Did you do your homework yesterday? _____

3 Have you been at home since this afternoon? _____

4 Did you eat all your breakfast this morning? _____

**24** Match the words with the definitions. Write the letters.

___ **1** conflict

**a** someone who writes reports for newspapers, magazines, TV, or radio

___ **2** peace

**b** to have the result you want

___ **3** journalist

**c** not supporting any country in a war, or any person in an argument

___ **4** succeed

**d** a disagreement or fighting

___ **5** neutral

**e** a situation in which there is no war, trouble, or fighting

**25** Listen and read. What is the purpose of Earthdance International?

# Imagine a World of Peace

Conflict happens everywhere. It happens in our homes, our schools, our friendships, and–certainly– in our world. When conflict happens, people start to "take sides." To take sides means to believe that one person, group, or opinion is completely right and the others are completely wrong. When people take sides, they often don't listen or hear the other side's opinions or concerns. Do you sometimes feel that someone isn't listening to you when you give your opinion or explain your ideas? How can you encourage people to really listen to you?

Can you imagine a world without conflict? Can you imagine a world where people live together peacefully? Earthdance International can. Earthdance International is an organization that was founded in 1997. Its purpose is to use music and dance to bring people and countries together for peace–especially countries taking sides against each other. Once a year, Earthdance International organizes the Global Festival for Peace. The Festival takes place in different countries around the world, at the same time, on the same day. It's "the largest global synchronized music and peace event in the world." It has taken place in over 80 countries as well as online! Musicians, singers, dancers, and artists from around the world come together to create song and dance. Journalists and representatives from many organizations talk about peaceful ways to end conflict, injustice, and environmental problems. Everyone enjoys the music and fun, but they're also hard at work discussing ways to make the world a better place. Everyone feels that being neutral to difficult problems is the first step toward success in finding peaceful solutions for them.

So, even though there is conflict all around the world, there are also organizations like Earthdance International that are trying to bring about peace and make the world a better place. What would you rather have–conflict or peace? What can you do to make your home, school, neighborhood, or country more peaceful? When you next face a difficult situation, can you think of a peaceful solution?

**26** Read **25** again and circle the correct answers.

**1** To "take sides" means to believe that one person, group or opinion is right and the others are _____ .

    **a** wrong                **b** right

**2** Earthdance International was founded in _____ .

    **a** 1987                **b** 1997

**3** Earthdance International organizes the Global Festival for Peace _____ .

    **a** twice a year                **b** once a year

**4** The festival takes place in different countries around the world, at the same time, _____ .

    **a** on the same day                **b** in the same place

**27** Complete the sentences with the words in the box.

conflict      injustice      opinion      organization      peace

**1** Seeds of Peace is an _____ that brings teenagers together to learn about how to make changes in their countries.

**2** _____ often happens in times of war when people are treated unfairly or badly by others.

**3** There is a _____ between the two countries, and their leaders are trying to hold peace talks.

**4** In my _____ , it is better to listen and to try to understand your enemies than to fight with them.

**5** There are many people around the world who are working hard to create _____ in difficult areas.

> Earthdance International invites people to get together to talk while dancing and listening to music. Why do you think the organization believes that dancing and music are important for creating peace?
>
> THINK BIG
>
> _____
>
> Would you like to join Earthdance International? Why/Why not?
>
> _____

In a biography, you write about the important events and details of someone's life. These can include:

- the place where someone was born
- the schools the person went to and what he or she studied
- the jobs the person had
- accomplishments
- important memories and people
- interests

It helps to ask questions and put the events in the correct order.

**28** Unscramble the questions. Imagine you are interviewing Stephen Hillenburg, the creator of *SpongeBob SquarePants*.

**1** born? / were / where / you

**You:** _____ ?

**Stephen:** I was born in Anaheim, California, in 1961.

**2** what / study / you / did / in college?

**You:** _____ ?

**Stephen:** I studied Marine Biology in college but I really wanted to study Art.

I got a Master of Fine Arts degree in animation in 1991.

**3** are / some / your / what / of / important memories?

**You:** _____ ?

**Stephen:** When I was young, I loved watching films about the sea. I loved drawing and painting, too.

**4** jobs / have / kinds of / what / you / had?

**You:** _____ ?

**Stephen:** I was a marine biologist from 1984 to 1987. I started working as an animator in 1991.

**5** what / your / some of / are / accomplishments?

**You:** _____ ?

**Stephen:** I've made many films but my biggest accomplishment is creating the cartoon *SpongeBob SquarePants* in 1999. In 2013, it won favorite cartoon of the year at the Kids' Choice Awards.

**29** Write a short biography of Stephen Hillenburg. Use the information in 28. Write two more questions. Do research and find the answers. Add the information to the biography.

**30** Complete the paragraphs. Use the correct form of the verbs in parentheses and for or since.

I have some amazing friends. I **1**_____ (know) my friend Anthony **2**_____ we were five years old. He **3**_____ (play) chess **4**_____ twelve years and he **5**_____ (win) many tournaments. I **6**_____ (try) to beat him **7**_____ many years, but I **8**_____ (not have) any luck! Besides being an amazing chess player, Anthony can also speak French! He **9**_____ (live) in France **10**_____ four years before coming to this country.

I **11**_____ (be) friends with Stella **12**_____ three years. She's an amazing musician. She **13**_____ (play) the piano **14**_____ she was four years old. Last year, she **15**_____ (play) in our school concert and she **16**_____ (be) amazing! She also loves science. She **17**_____ (be) a member of our school's science club **18**_____ more than two years.

**31** Look at 30. Then answer the questions.

1 Has Anthony won many tournaments? _____

2 Did Anthony live in France for three years? _____

3 Has Stella played the piano for two years? _____

4 Did Stella play in the school concert last year? _____

**32** Answer the questions. Use the present perfect continuous and since.

1 *SpongeBob SquarePants* started in 1999. How long has he been making children laugh?

_____

2 Seeds of Peace started in 1993. How long has Seeds of Peace been offering its training to teenagers?

_____

# DILEMMAS

**1** Look at the pictures. How do you think the people are feeling? Write the numbers.

| **1** angry | **2** worried | **3** upset |
|---|---|---|
| **4** guilty | **5** happy | **6** in trouble |
| **7** good about himself or herself | | |

**2** Look at **1**. What do you think has happened to the people? Why do they look this way? Choose one person and ✔ all possible answers. Add three of your own ideas.

The person...

☐ cheated in a test                     ☐ heard a hurtful lie

☐ helped a friend at school             ☐ stopped a bully

☐ had a fight with a friend             ☐ _____

☐ _____              ☐ _____

**3** Complete the dialogs. Circle the correct words.

**1 Kate:** Yesterday, I borrowed my mom's jacket but I lost it at the park. I don't want her to **get into trouble / be upset** with me so I'm going to tell her that someone else took it.

**Sally:** Why don't you check the lost property office? Maybe someone found the jacket and took it there. Then you can **feel guilty / tell the truth** and **feel good / return** the jacket to your mom.

**2 Jim:** My mom asked me who took the money that was on the table. I told her my little brother took it. And now he's going to **tell the truth / get into trouble** and I don't **feel guilty / feel good** about it.

**Sam:** You should tell your mom the truth, Jim. If you tell the truth, it'll be OK. And tell your brother that you're sorry. But who took the money?

**Jim:** I don't know.

**4** Read the dilemma. What do you think? Complete the sentences. Use your own ideas.

You and your friend find an expensive jacket at the bus stop. There's a wallet in the pocket with an address in it. Your friend takes the jacket and returns it to the owner. The owner gives your friend a reward of $50. Your friend keeps the money and doesn't say anything to you. Then you find out the truth.

**1** How do you feel?

I _____.

**2** How should your friend feel?

My friend _____.

**3** How do you think your friend feels?

My friend probably _____.

**4** What should your friend have done?

My friend should have _____.

**THINK BIG**

Have you had a dilemma recently? What was it? How did you feel? What happened in the end?

_____

_____

**5** Listen and read. Circle the correct answers.

# GARY'S DILEMMA

Gary was walking out of school when his best friend Ryan ran up to him. "We're OK, right? If my mom calls you, you'll say it's true that I'm studying with you, right?" he whispered. Behind Ryan stood Max and a gang of boys Gary didn't want to know.

Gary nodded, trying to smile.

"Come on, Ryan, let's go!" Max called.

"Just a sec!" Ryan said. He turned back to Gary. "Thanks, Gary. See you soon, OK?"

"Yeah, sure," said Gary and he turned and headed for home. How did this happen? He should have said no in the first place.

"Hey, Gary! Wait!" Gary turned and saw Pete running towards him.

"Hi, Pete," said Gary, without looking at Pete.

"What's up with you?" Pete said.

"Sorry," said Gary, "I'm just thinking about something."

"By the way," Pete said, "what's up with Ryan? What's he doing hanging out with Max and those other guys? That gang's always getting into trouble!"

"I don't know but he can do whatever he wants," shrugged Gary.

Pete grabbed Gary's shoulder. "I can't believe you said that! Ryan's our friend. If he's in trouble, we should help him."

Gary looked down, thinking, *If I tell, Ryan will think he can't trust me and I might lose him as a friend. I don't want to be in trouble with the gang, either. But if I don't tell, something terrible might happen to Ryan.* Gary had to make a decision.

1 Ryan and Gary **are / aren't** going to study together.

2 Gary **is / isn't** going to tell a lie to Ryan's mom.

3 Max and his gang **are / aren't** friends of Gary's.

4 Pete thinks he and Gary **have to / don't have** to do something to help Ryan.

**6** Answer the questions. Use your own ideas.

1 Why do children join gangs? Why do you think Ryan joined the gang?

_____

2 What should Gary and Pete do?

_____

**7** **Listen and read. Then answer the questions.**

**Mom:**      <u>What's the matter</u>, Chris?

**Chris:**     Nothing, Mom.

**Mom:**      Did something happen at school today?

**Chris:**     Well... yeah... but it's not important.

**Mom:**      <u>Look</u>. If you don't tell me what's wrong, I can't help you. Tell me <u>what's going on</u>.

**Chris:**     Well, a couple of boys at school are <u>being mean</u> to me.

**Mom:**      Are they? Did they hurt you?

**Chris:**     No, it's nothing like that. They just <u>call me names</u> sometimes.

**Mom:**      I'm glad you told me, Chris. Let's think about what you can do.

**1**  What is Chris's dilemma? _____

**2**  What does Chris's mom want him to do? _____

**3**  Why do you think Chris doesn't want to talk to his mom about his problem? _____

_____

**8** **Look at 7. Read the underlined expressions. Match and write the letter.**

___**1**  What's the matter?          **a**  They're unkind and cruel.

___**2**  Look.                        **b**  What's up?

___**3**  They're being mean.         **c**  Listen.

___**4**  They call me names.         **d**  What's wrong?

___**5**  What's going on?            **e**  They tease and insult me.

**9** **Answer the questions.**

**1**  Why do you think the boys at school are being mean to Chris?

_____

**2**  What would you say to someone if he or she called you names?

_____

# Language in Action

> If he **pays attention** in class, he**'ll understand** the lesson.
>
> If they **don't study** for the math test, they **won't get** a good grade.
>
> If you **tell** me the truth, I**'ll help** you.

I can't be late!

**10** **Unscramble the phrases to complete the sentences.**

**1** am / late / for / If / I / school /
_____, I'll have to go to the office.

**2** my friend Jimmy / see / I / will
If I go to the office, _____. He's always late.

**3** see / If / my friend Jimmy / I
_____, we'll start talking about manga comics because we always do.

**4** will / going back / forget about / we / to our classroom
If we start talking about manga comics, _____.

**5** shout / The head teacher / at us / will
_____ if he sees us talking in the corridor.

**6** a / is / he / bad mood / If / in
_____, he'll make us stay after school.

**11** **Match the sentences. Write the letter.**

____ **1** My friend lends me a video game.

____ **2** I don't do my chores.

____ **3** A classmate cheats on a test.

____ **4** I tell my friend that I lied to him.

____ **5** I don't study.

**a** He gets upset.

**b** I take really good care of it.

**c** The teacher calls the parents.

**d** I don't pass the test.

**e** I apologize to my parents.

**12** **Write sentences using the ideas in 11. Use If.**

**1** _____

**2** _____

**3** _____

**4** _____

**5** _____

> You **should tell** your parents **if** you have a problem at school.
>
> **If** you don't want to get into trouble, you **shouldn't lie**.

**13** Read the advice column. Complete the sentences with the correct form of the words in the box. Add should if necessary.

| call | find | give | say | start | stop | tell (x2) |

## Ask Jenna and Jack: Smart Advice for Kids

Dear Jenna,

My friend keeps calling me names like "stupid" and "idiot." She always apologizes later but it makes me upset. I asked her to stop but she won't. What should I do?

Sad Samantha

Dear Sad Samantha,

This girl is NOT your friend! If this girl _____ you names again, you _____ her to apologize immediately. If she _____ no, you _____ a new friend!

Jenna

Dear Jack,

My little brother's always following me around. I feel guilty when I tell him to stop because he cries but I don't want him hanging around. My friends don't like it either. What should I do?

Guilty Gordon

Dear Guilty Gordon,

This is a difficult problem. Arrange times to play with your little brother. Then tell him that he can't follow you with your friends. If he _____ to follow you and your friends, _____ him to stop. Tell him that you and he will play together later. If he _____ following you, _____ him a reward. Good luck!

Jack

**14** Complete the sentences with advice. Use should or shouldn't.

1 If you borrow something from a friend, _____.

2 If someone is mean to you, _____.

3 If you have a problem at school, _____.

**15** Read and ✔.

**1** good enough

   **a** harmless ☐       **b** acceptable ☐

**2** rules that people use to decide what behavior is right and what is wrong

   **a** ethics ☐       **b** moral ☐

**3** relating to ideas about what behavior is right and wrong

   **a** respectful ☐       **b** ethical ☐

**4** qualities that are part of a person's character

   **a** ethics ☐       **b** traits ☐

**5** a way of thinking about something; a point of view

   **a** morally ☐       **b** perspective ☐

**6** to behave toward someone in a particular way

   **a** treat ☐       **b** trait ☐

**16** Listen and read. What does "character" mean?

| Ethics |
|---|
| **1 Ethics** is knowing what good and bad behavior is. You make choices based on ethics about what's **morally** right or wrong, or what's fair or unfair. |
| **2** Your **character** is all of your **traits** and qualities taken together, such as being friendly, honest, and hard-working. |
| **3 Treat** means how you act towards others. Do you **treat** people nicely or are you mean? |
| **4 Ethical behavior** is when you do the right thing and treat someone fairly and respectfully. Ethical behavior is good and fair behavior, which is acceptable in a given situation. |
| **5** It is important to try to see things from the right **perspective**, so that we understand things well and make good decisions. |
| **6** You should always try to behave in an **acceptable** way, so that you don't upset or harm yourself or others. |

**17** Read 16 again and circle the correct answers.

**1** Sam is serious, clever, sometimes mean to others, and impatient. These words describe ___.

   **a** character                    **b** ethics

**2** You can treat someone badly or well. *Treat* means ___.

   **a** the way you act with someone    **b** the way you think about someone

**3** Look at the two behaviors below. The ethical behavior is ___.

   **a** you see someone hurt a classmate and    **b** you see someone hurt a classmate
   you don't tell because you're afraid         and you tell a teacher

**4** When you have a problem and you think about the right and wrong ways to act, you're thinking about ___.

   **a** character                    **b** ethics

**18** Unscramble and write. Then make up a sentence with each word.

**1** _____ srecepftlu

_____

**2** _____ hetcial

_____

**3** _____ rpepscevtie

_____

**4** _____ roamlyl

_____

**5** _____ cacpetleab

_____

**6** _____ ratet

_____

**THINK BIG** How do you decide what's right and what's wrong? Are there questions that you ask yourself to decide? What are they? Answer in your notebook.

## Grammar

**19** Read and match. Write the letters.

___ 1 If I cheat on the test,

___ 2 If you fall and hurt yourself,

___ 3 If he doesn't tell his mother,

___ 4 If they go too far,

___ 5 If we tell lies,

___ 6 If she behaves well,

___ 7 If Daphne stays up too late,

___ 8 If you don't like loud people,

a   they may get lost.

b   my teacher will fail me.

c   we could get in trouble.

d   you should go to the first aid room.

e   she may go to the party.

f   he might tell his father.

g   you should ask them to talk more quietly.

h   she may not wake up in time.

**20** Read and circle.

1   If she buys the necklace, she **may / may not** spend all her money.

2   If you see an ambulance, you **should / should not** move out of the way.

3   If they don't practice every day, they **might / might not** improve.

4   If he doesn't tell his grandma about the broken lamp, she **may / may not** get very cross.

5   If we see elephants in the wild, we **should / should not** make a loud noise.

6   If I go to Paris in the summer, I **could / could not** see the Eiffel Tower.

**21** Complete the sentences with the words in the box.

> If   might   should not   work   should

1 _____ you run across the road, you may get knocked over.

2 If I hear a strange noise, I _____ tell my parents.

3 If she doesn't _____ hard at school, she may not pass her exams.

4 If we are very quiet, we _____ hear some unusual animal sounds.

5 If they are late, they _____ walk home in the dark.

**22** Complete the sentences. Use will, may, might, could, or should.

1 If I am late for school, _____.

2 If we don't get up early, _____.

3 If you go hiking, _____.

4 If they don't catch the thief, _____.

5 If she visits her cousins in Madrid, _____.

6 If Daniel doesn't forget his books, _____.

**23** Complete the sentences. Use If + present simple tense.

1 _____
_____,
you might get ill.

2 _____
_____,
they could visit the art gallery.

3 _____,
_____,
she won't watch the film.

4 _____
_____,
we might not arrive on time.

5 _____
_____,
I will stay up late.

6 _____
_____,
he should wash his hands.

**24** Match the proverbs with their meanings. Write the letters.

___ **1** "A clear conscience (mind) is a soft pillow."

___ **2** "Better to be alone than to be in bad company."

___ **3** "A friend's eye is a good mirror."

**a** I don't need friends if they aren't good ones.

**b** I trust my friends to tell me the truth about myself.

**c** If I don't tell the truth, I won't feel good about myself (and might not be able to sleep at night).

 50 **25** Listen and read. Match the stories with the proverbs above. Write 1, 2, or 3.

# Problems and Proverbs

All around the world, in every culture, people use proverbs to explain things about life or human nature. Proverbs are short sayings that give advice and help us to make decisions. Some proverbs tell us about ourselves and our friends, as in the three stories below about friendships.

**Dilemma A:** ___
Nellie is a new girl at school. She's very shy so she finds it hard to make friends. A group of girls asks Nellie if she wants to be friends with them. Nellie is very happy to say yes. She feels like she's part of a group and is happy because the girls are fun to be with. But Nellie begins to notice that these girls are loud in class and don't pay much attention to the teacher. The girls notice that Nellie is good at math. They ask her to do their math homework. They say that if she doesn't, they'll tell lies about her. Nellie feels very hurt. She tells the girls that she won't be their friend anymore. The girls tell lies about Nellie but Nellie doesn't care. She walks alone to school and feels good about herself.

**Dilemma B:** ___
Doug hasn't been doing his homework. He's stopped hanging out with his friends. He just wants to make robots and listen to music. He keeps making promises to people but he never keeps them. Today, he was supposed to help Calvin fix his bike but he didn't. Calvin stops by Doug's house. He says that Doug isn't acting like a friend. He's not being responsible. Calvin tells Doug that he should talk to his parents or to a teacher at school. Doug gets really angry and says that Calvin is stupid. Calvin leaves. Doug thinks about his behavior and realizes that Calvin is probably right. Calvin's a good friend.

**Dilemma C:** ___
Gloria and Zoe are Tina's best friends. They tell Tina that they stole some bracelets at the craft fair at school last Saturday. Tina's teacher thinks she saw Donna near the bracelets so now everyone thinks that Donna took them. Tina doesn't know Donna well but she feels awful. Gloria and Zoe beg Tina not to tell anyone. They say they won't do it again. Tina feels very guilty. She decides to tell the truth anyway. She feels good about the decision but very sad about her friends. She hopes they understand and that they can stay friends. She knows they just made a stupid mistake.

**26** Read 25 again and circle T for true or F for false.

| | | | |
|---|---|---|---|
| **1** | Proverbs give advice and help us make decisions. | T | F |
| **2** | Nellie is loud and outgoing. | T | F |
| **3** | Nellie prefers to be alone than to have bad friends. | T | F |
| **4** | Doug is responsible and good at keeping promises. | T | F |
| **5** | Calvin is not a good friend to Doug. | T | F |
| **6** | Tina tells the truth about what her friends did. | T | F |

**27** Unscramble and write the proverbs. Then read and ✔.

**1**  reap / sow / what / you'll / you

_____

**a** you get what you give ☐          **b** it's time to collect things ☐

**2**  crocodiles / just because / don't think / the water / there are no / is calm

_____

**a** even if something seems safe,          **b** don't go in the water with crocodiles ☐
there could be danger ☐

**3**  the camel / the couscous / little by litte / goes into

_____

**a** eat slowly ☐          **b** everything happens in its own time ☐

Describe something that has happened in your life that relates to one of the proverbs in this lesson. (Write the proverb and then describe what happened.)

**THINK BIG**

_____

_____

_____

_____

# Writing | Story Ending

A well-written story ends in a way that seems "right" or possible for the main character. Here are ways to help you decide what endings are "right" or possible:

- Find information in the story about the character's traits.
- Notice how the character treats others.
- Look at the character's actions and feelings.

**28** Read *Gary's Dilemma* on page 34 again. Circle the traits that describe Gary's character.

| caring | funny | honest | lazy | mean | not honest | serious | worried |

**29** Complete the sentences about Gary. Include one of the traits you circled in 28 and ideas from the story. Use the ideas in the box or your own ideas.

asks his parents what he should do      says nothing and hopes that Ryan is OK
talks to the gang members      tells a teacher about Ryan
tells Ryan he should stop hanging around with the gang      tells Ryan's parents

I think that Gary is _____ (trait) because in the story he _____
_____ .
It's possible that he'll _____ .
I don't think that Gary will _____ .

**30** Think about Gary's character. What does he do the next day? Think about these questions.

What is the first thing that he does? What happens to Gary and Ryan? Are they still friends? Why/Why not?

**31** Write an ending to *Gary's Dilemma* on another piece of paper. Look at 28, 29, and 30 to help you. Begin: *The next day, Gary made a decision.*

THINK BIG

Everybody makes mistakes. When we make a mistake, what should we do? Why?

_____
_____

**32** Match the expressions with the situations. Write the letters.

___ **1** tell the truth

___ **2** feel guilty

___ **3** cheat

___ **4** feel good

___ **5** get into trouble

___ **6** be upset with

**a** Amy looked at Suzie's test and copied the answers.

**b** Steve's mom is angry with him because he didn't do his homework.

**c** Meg feels bad because she hurt Evan's feelings.

**d** Mike hit Ryan on the playground and he had to go to the principal's office.

**e** Jeff said that Claire took the money. She did.

**f** Monica helped Robert study for his test. She's happy she could help him.

**33** Write what will happen. Use will and the words in parentheses.

**1** Maya knows her brother cheated on a test. She wants to <u>tell her parents</u>. What will her brother do? (be / angry)

_____

**2** Janet stole some money from her mom. She wants to <u>apologize to her mom</u>. What will her mom do? (say / disappointed)

_____

**3** Ivy got into trouble because she was with a group of girls who called a young boy names and made him cry. She wants to <u>apologize</u>. What will he probably do? (say / OK)

_____

**Unscramble the words. Complete the phrases.**

## SCHOOL ACTIVITIES

1  hand in an _____
2  do _____
3  study for a _____
4  pay _____
5  be more _____

_____ttse_____   _____

_____   _____atttionen_____

_____hmwokroe_____   _____

_____   _____ssaey_____

_____cfulare_____   _____

_____   _____saekp_____

_____pbishlu_____   _____

_____   _____cblmi_____

_____boemec_____   _____

_____   _____teme_____

## REACHING GOALS

1  _____ a book
2  _____ a doctor
3  _____ two languages
4  _____ a world leader
5  _____ a mountain

## MAKING CHOICES

1  _____ on a test
2  _____ guilty
3  be _____
4  _____ the truth
5  get into _____

_____tspeu_____   _____

_____   _____toruble_____

_____fele_____   _____

_____   _____eltl_____

_____cetah_____   _____

**2** Find a song that makes you think about school days, goals, or dilemmas. Complete the chart.

Song Title _____

Singer's or group's name _____

What language is used in the song? _____

How long have you liked this singer/group? _____

How long has this singer/group been performing? _____

What's the song about? _____

What happens in the song? _____

_____

If you can change words (lyrics) in the

song, which lyrics will you change? _____

_____

**3** Draw pictures to illustrate your song. Then write the story of your song on a separate piece of paper.

# unit 4
# DREAMS FOR THE FUTURE

**1** Match the pictures with the predictions. Check (✓) when you think the predictions may come true.

| Predictions for the Future | Now | In My Lifetime | Never |
|---|---|---|---|
| ___ Spaceships to other planets will be departing daily. | | | |
| ___ Robots will be teaching in the classroom. | | | |
| ___ People around the world will be living happily together. | | | |
| ___ We'll be driving flying cars. | | | |
| ___ We'll be making progress towards finding cures for many serious diseases. | | | |

**2** Look at **1**. Explain one of your predictions.

_____

_____

**3** Match each picture with a phrase.

In the future, I'll be...

living in another country

working in my dream job

earning a good salary

running my own business

bringing up a family

Bonjour!

Wie geht es dir?

How are you?

**4** Complete the sentences with the words in 3.

1 In 20 years, I'll be _____. I really want children!

2 In 10 years, I'll be _____. I'll be a cartoonist. I've always wanted to draw cartoons. It'll be perfect!

3 In 10 years, I'll be _____ and I won't worry about money.

4 In 20 years, I'll be _____. I won't work for anyone. I'll be the boss!

5 In 10 years, I'll be _____. I'm not sure where. Maybe I'll be living in Germany.

**5** Unscramble the words to complete the sentences. Are they true or false for you? Circle T for true or F for false.

1 be / my / won't / I / running / own business          T          F
  In 20 years, _____.

2 a family / won't / I / bringing up / be /          T          F
  In 10 years, _____.

**THINK BIG**

Do you think the world will be a better or worse place 30 years from now? Why/Why not?

_____

_____

**6** Listen and read the e-mail. Then ✔ the predictions Christina makes about her classmates.

| TO | classmatesall@school.org |
|---|---|
| CC | |
| SUBJECT | Christina's Predictions |

Dear 6th grade students,

As class blogger, it's my job to write about our experiences as 6th grade students. I've been thinking a lot about my future lately and, since you know how curious and nosey I am, I can't help but think about your futures, too. It's never too early to think about what we'll be doing 10 or 20 years from now. I thought it'd be fun to start the conversation. This is what I predict:

I'll start with me. I know that in 10 years, I'll be running my own business in the fashion industry. That doesn't surprise you, does it?! You know how I love fashion and I also love being the boss! One thing I won't be doing is living in this city! I want to live abroad—maybe in Tokyo or Paris. Now, what about Jessie? I think he'll be working in his dream job as a cartoonist because that's all I see him doing at school. I bet he'll be making animated films. In 10 years, Stephanie will definitely be working in the music industry. She has an amazing voice. Don't you agree? George will be taking adventurous trips abroad because he'll be a famous journalist. He's very smart and he works so hard. I hope that all of my predictions come true!

That's not all but that's all I have time for now. If you want to reply, let me know your dreams and I'll add them to the school blog. Let's all think about our dreams and reach for the stars this year!

Your class blogger,

Christina

**Predictions**

☐ **1** working in his dream job          ☐ **2** living in this city

☐ **3** working in the music industry     ☐ **4** speaking foreign languages

☐ **5** earning a good salary             ☐ **6** married

☐ **7** famous                            ☐ **8** taking adventurous trips

**7** Make a prediction about what you'll be doing in 20 years and explain why.

I'll be _____ because _____.

**8** Listen and read. Then circle the answers.

**Jack:** What do you think you'll be doing after you finish school, Sandra?

**Sandra:** College, I'm sure. How about you? What will you be doing in, say, 15 years?

**Jack:** I'll be working on a big movie!

**Sandra:** A movie? You think you'll be a movie star?

**Jack:** No, not a movie star. A movie director. I'll be working with all the big Hollywood stars.

**Sandra:** Really? And how will you do that?

**Jack:** Well, I'm quite good at making short movies on my computer already. I just need one <u>big break</u>! I'll be the next Steven Spielberg!

**Sandra:** Right. I just hope you won't forget us when you're rich and famous!

**Jack:** Of course not! You and Mom will be walking <u>on the red carpet</u> with me!

**Sandra:** Oh, I like that idea!

**1** What does Jack think he'll be doing in 15 years?

   **a** He'll be acting in movies.   **b** He'll be directing movies.   **c** He'll be at college.

**2** Young actors and singers are always looking for a big break in their career. What does "big break" mean?

   **a** a big rest          **b** a chance to be          **c** a chance to travel
                                successful

**3** When an actor is "on the red carpet," what is he or she invited to attend?

   **a** an awards ceremony     **b** college          **c** a reading of the
                                                        film script

**9** Read the dialog in 8 again. Does Jack think he'll be successful? Why/Why not?

_____

_____

_____

_____

# Language in Action

| What **will** you **be doing** 10 years from now? | I'll definitely **be studying** at a big university. |
| Where **will** you **be living** in 20 years? | I probably **won't be living** in Europe. |

**10** Match. Then answer the questions. Use the future progressive of the verbs and the word in parentheses.

## Hopes and Dreams in 20 years

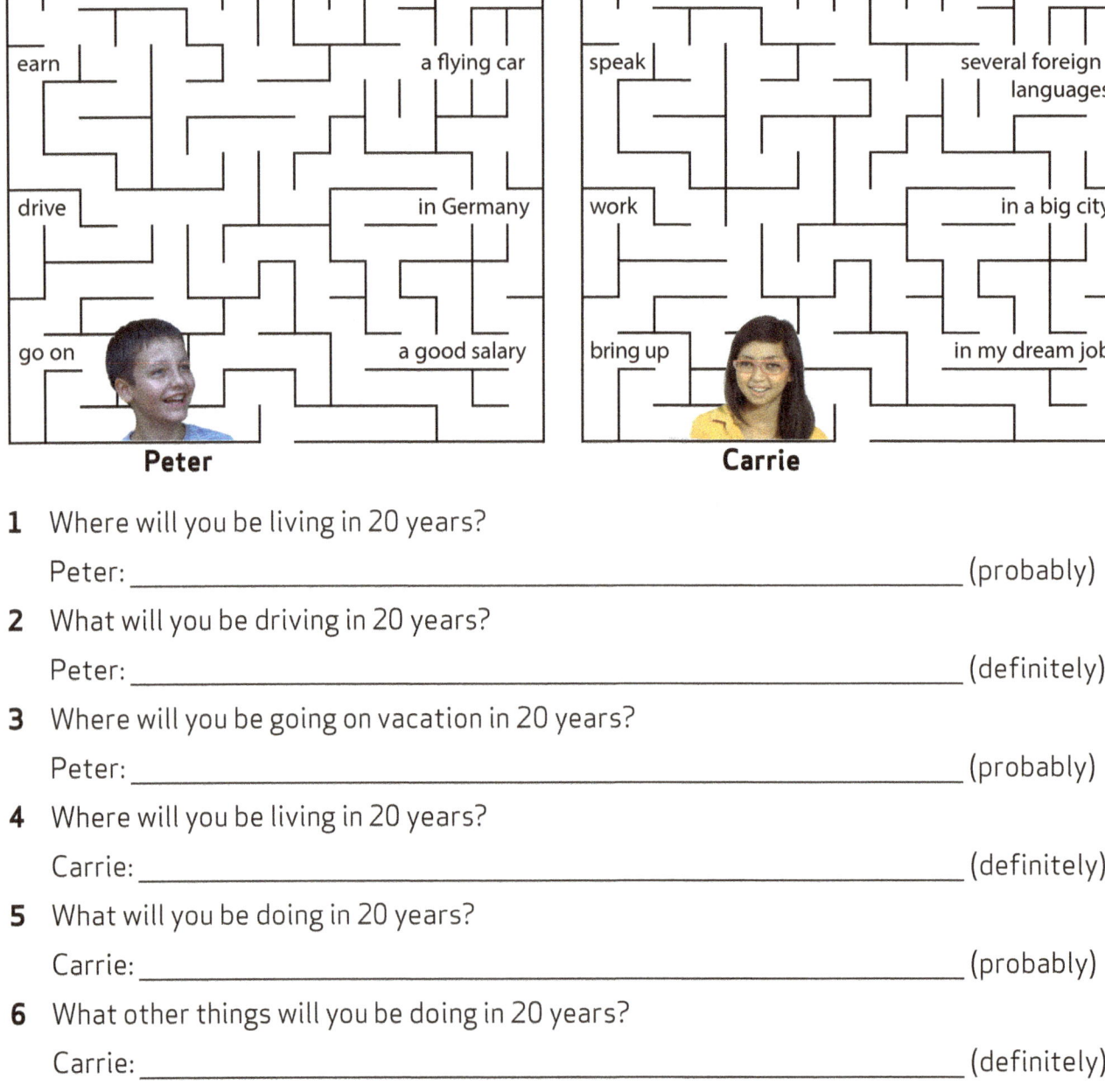

| | |
| --- | --- |
| live | vacation in the Caribbean |
| earn | a flying car |
| drive | in Germany |
| go on | a good salary |

**Peter**

| | |
| --- | --- |
| live | a family |
| speak | several foreign languages |
| work | in a big city |
| bring up | in my dream job |

**Carrie**

1   Where will you be living in 20 years?

Peter: _____ (probably)

2   What will you be driving in 20 years?

Peter: _____ (definitely)

3   Where will you be going on vacation in 20 years?

Peter: _____ (probably)

4   Where will you be living in 20 years?

Carrie: _____ (definitely)

5   What will you be doing in 20 years?

Carrie: _____ (probably)

6   What other things will you be doing in 20 years?

Carrie: _____ (definitely)

| **Will** you **be running** a business? | No, definitely not. I definitely **won't**… |
| | Yes, definitely. I definitely **will**… |
| | Probably not. I probably **won't**… |
| | Yes, probably. I probably **will**… |

**11** Answer the questions. Use the information in 10.

1 Will Carrie be working in her dream job in 20 years?

_____

2 Will Peter be living in Germany in 20 years?

_____

3 Will Carrie be living in a small city in 20 years?

_____

4 Will Peter be going on vacation in Asia in 20 years?

_____

5 Will Carrie be bringing up a family in 20 years?

_____

6 Will Peter be driving a flying car in 20 years?

_____

**12** Answer the questions about your future life at college with No, definitely not, Yes, definitely, or Probably not.

1 Will you be seeing your family a lot when you go to college?

_____

2 Will you be studying a foreign language at college?

_____

3 Will you be studying harder than you do now?

_____

**13** Choose a friend. Write a question about your friend's future at college. Ask your friend the question. Then write the answer No, definitely not, Yes, definitely, or Probably not.

Q: _____

A: _____

**14**  Read and ✔.

1  someone who studies the future    **a** nanobot ☐    **b** futurist ☐
2  not real, but imagined    **a** imaginary ☐    **b** virtual ☐
3  extremely small    **a** microscopic ☐    **b** wireless ☐
4  to change the way people think or act    **a** treat ☐    **b** revolutionize ☐
5  the science of extremely small things    **a** 3-D ☐    **b** nanotechnology ☐
6  pictures and sounds that simulate places    **a** virtual reality ☐    **b** 3-D ☐

**15**  64  Read and complete with the words in the box. Then listen and check.

| imagine | nanotechnology | robots | 3-D | virtual | wireless |

# Two Trends in Medicine

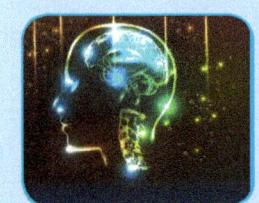

Futurists, whose job is to study the future and help people to prepare for the future, are talking about two important trends in the future of medicine. A trend is the way something is developing or changing, and these two trends in medicine may revolutionize the way illnesses and diseases are diagnosed and treated by doctors in the future.

One important trend in the future of medicine is [1]_____. The word nano means billionth. That's really tiny! Scientists who are working in nanotechnology are studying particles that are so small that they are invisible to the human eye! In fact, they have to measure these particles with a new unit of measurement, called the nanometer. Do you see the word "meter" in nanometer? You know how long a meter is, don't you?

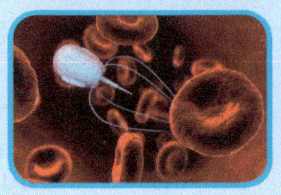

Can you [2]_____ something that is only 1/1,000,000,000 of a baseball bat? One example of this is the nanobot. These microscopic robots are made of the same material that we are made of: DNA. In the future, scientists will be using nanobots to treat diseases and illnesses. For example, when you become ill in the future, doctors will put a nanobot into your body. The robot will find the cause of your illness and give you the correct medicine to help it heal. Wouldn't that be great? Think about it: When you become ill, your insides will be like a video game: [3]_____ will be searching for the "baddies" and destroying them.

The second trend in the future is in [4]_____ medicine. Thirty years from now, when you have a fever and feel ill, you won't have to leave the house and go to a doctor. You'll be using [5]_____ technology to diagnose and treat your illness in your own home. In this futuristic scenario, you'll take [6]_____ pictures of your body using an object like a TV remote control. You'll upload these images to a website. The doctor will download the images, review them, and upload medicine for you to download. If the doctor wants to talk to you, he or she will talk to you through a video call – or maybe he or she will "visit" you using 3-D technology. The doctor will look like he or she is in your house but it will just be a 3-D image. Wouldn't that be amazing?

The future of medicine promises to revolutionize the way illnesses and diseases are diagnosed and treated, as well as the way in which we interact with doctors. Do you think we are ready for this?

**16** Read 15 again and circle the correct answers.

1 The word "nano" means a ____ .

   **a** millionth        **b** billionth

2 In the future, doctors may put a ____ inside your body.

   **a** nanobot        **b** toy robot

3 In the future, a doctor will look at 3-D ____ of your body in order to treat you.

   **a** objects        **b** images

4 Virtual medicine makes use of wireless ____ in your home.

   **a** technology        **b** pictures

**17** Complete the sentences with words from 14.

1 There are two trends in medicine that promise to _____ the way people's illnesses are diagnosed and treated.

2 _____ involves the study of extremely tiny particles, which are invisible to the human eye.

3 _____ enables someone to enter an _____ world on the computer where places, objects, and people seem almost real.

4 Nanobots are _____ robots that can be put inside our bodies to find the cause of our illnesses and help people to heal.

5 A _____ is someone who predicts the future and assists with planning for it.

**THINK BIG**

Think about the size of things around you. The head of a pin is 1,000,000 (one million) nanometers wide. What's the size of these objects in nanometers? Guess and complete with the numbers in the box.

> 2 billion      5,000,000      100,000

An ant is about _____ nanometers wide.

A human hair is about _____ nanometers wide.

A man who is two meters tall is about _____ nanometers tall.

# Grammar

**18** Read and circle.

1 I **said** / **say** that I would get up early.

2 The scientist said **that** / **what** robots could be used in medicine.

3 He said that nanotechnology **did** / **would** revolutionize the world as we know it.

4 Futurists **say** / **said** we needed to prepare for the future.

5 We said we wanted to know more about virtual technology and how it **would** / **has** be used responsibly.

**19** Read and match.

1 "I **study** computer technology at college."

2 "She works in an office in central London."

3 "I read the latest science magazine every day."

4 "We are going to Italy in the summer."

5 "They live in a small house with a big yard."

6 "We love learning about future technology."

a They said they were going to Italy in the summer.

b Dan said that they lived in a small house with a big yard.

c The students said they loved learning about future technology.

d I said that I **studied** computer technology at college.

e They said that she worked in an office in central London.

f My friend said that he read the latest science magazine every day.

**20** Complete the sentences with the words in the box.

> understood    played    said    that    would

1 My sister _____ that math and science were her best subjects at school.
2 His mother said that he _____ virtual games on his computer all afternoon.
3 Frank said _____ architects made 3-D images of houses they were building.
4 We said no one _____ what the scientist was talking about.
5 They said that they _____ like to learn more about virtual medicine.

**21** Unscramble and write the sentences.

1 I needed to study / said that / computer technology / my father

_____

2 watch TV / for an hour / she wanted to / she said

_____

3 said that / assists doctors / futurists / nanobots would

_____

4 would revolutionize / that / she said / it / the future

_____

**22** Write the sentences in reported speech. Use said or said that.

1 Ana: "Robots are used to help humans do new things."

_____

2 Josh: "The study of the future is very interesting."

_____

3 My grandfather: "So many things are different now."

_____

4 Mary: "I will read my book instead of playing a computer game."

_____

**23** Read and match. Write the letters.

| | | | | |
|---|---|---|---|---|
| 1 ___ manual | | **a** | the fact that someone is male or female |
| 2 ___ harmoniously | | **b** | no longer living or active |
| 3 ___ extinct | | **c** | your general attitude toward life |
| 4 ___ space shuttle | | **d** | done without conflict |
| 5 ___ gender | | **e** | a plane that can go into space and back |
| 6 ___ outlook | | **f** | done by hand |

**24** Listen and read. What did the children want the computers to look and act like?

## Young Inventors

What will your future look like? It depends on the inventions that inventors are dreaming up today, doesn't it? And who are those inventors? You might think that inventors are old people who have worked for many years on their ideas. That may have been what inventors looked like years ago, but in this technological age, that view of inventors is becoming extinct.

Researchers today think the ideas for inventions will come from children. They recently interviewed children, aged 12 and under, from all around the world and asked them what they thought computers would be like in the future. They were amazed by how many wonderful and inventive ideas the children talked about. These children were very comfortable with technology and they wanted to see computers do more and more for them. In fact, the children wanted computers to look and act human. They didn't think it would be strange to have a computer as a friend! They had some differences of opinion about what exactly they wanted computers to do. Some children said they wanted computers that would play with them and help them with homework. Other children wanted to use computers to learn new skills and do things more easily, like speaking a foreign language. Others wanted to use computers to create things like video games and virtual-reality places. Many children also wanted computers to do more things at school and at home for them—like making learning more interesting or helping them with chores.

Everyone thought it would be great if they could mix online and real-life experiences harmoniously. For example, they wanted to be able to see things online—like a sandwich—and make it into a real sandwich using a machine like a printer. Or choose a new pair of jeans or sneakers and then turn them into the real items. Or even design their own toy and then change it into a real toy that they could play with. Sounds cool, doesn't it?

What do you think about these ideas? Do you agree that children like you will be creating new inventions for the future? Do you think children have a fresher outlook on life and a better understanding of technology than adults, which enables them to be the inventors of the future? Maybe you have an idea for an invention. Perhaps it's an idea for something at home or at school. If you do, draw it, write about it, and tell someone! You might be the next Steve Jobs!

**25** Read 24 again and correct the sentences.

1 In this technological age, the ideas for inventions come from old people.

_____

2 Researchers recently interviewed children, aged 12 and over, about what computers would be like in the future.

_____

3 The children had many differences of opinion about what they wanted computers to do.

_____

4 Not everyone agreed it would be great to mix online and real-life experiences.

_____

**26** Complete the sentences with the words in the box.

invention    inventor    online    opinion    technological

1 Children talked about the _____ of smartphones more than 20 years ago.
2 Researchers predict that most _____ inventions will be created by children.
3 My sister wants to be an _____ of technological gadgets for the home.
4 You can buy and order so many things _____ today, like air tickets and groceries.
5 In their _____, it is worth asking young people what they think the future will be like.

THINK BIG

The children had different ideas about computers. What would you like computers to do in the future?

_____

_____

_____

When you write an e-mail, you need to think about who you're writing to. If you're writing to a teacher or other adult, you'll write a formal e-mail. If you're writing to a friend, you'll write an informal e-mail. Here are some ways these two kinds of e-mails are different.

|  | Formal E-mail | Informal E-mail |
|---|---|---|
| **1 Subject** | 1 Be clear and specific. *This week's essay* | 1 Write something simple. *Tonight* or *Hi* |
| **2 Greeting** | 2 Use Ms. / Mr. / Mrs. *Mrs. Smith,* | 2 Write *Hi, Tony,* or *Hey, Tony,* |
| **3 Body** | 3 Write your message in full sentences, check your spelling, and be polite. *I missed school yesterday because I was ill. Can you tell me what the homework is, please?* | 3 u can use short words coz u wanna write quickly to ur bff. |
| **4 Closing** | 4 Write *Yours sincerely* or *Best wishes* and your name below. | 4 Write your name. |

**27** Read each sentence. Write formal if it belongs in a formal e-mail or informal if it belongs in an informal e-mail.

1 _____ Hey, Tami,

2 _____ I am having trouble deciding what to do for my science project. Could you help me think of some ideas?

3 _____ c u later bff!

4 _____ Dear Mr. Taylor,

5 _____ Yours sincerely, Steve

**28** Write formal and informal e-mails on a separate piece of paper. In the informal e-mail, use abbreviations from the Tips box.

**Tips**

**Texting Abbreviations**

b4 = before

bff = best friends forever

c = see

coz = because

gonna = going to

TTYL = talk to you later

u = you

wanna = want to

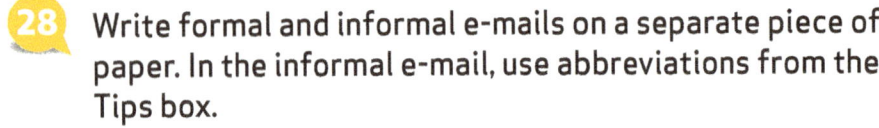

Why do we use different language, formal and informal, when talking to different people?

THINK
BIG

_____

_____

**29** **Complete the sentences. Use the future progressive of the verbs in parentheses.**

Chris and his sister, Ann, have big plans for the future. Chris **1**_____

probably _____ (go) to college in 10 years. Once he graduates, he

**2**_____ (work) as a businessman with his dad. He definitely **3**_____

(not live) in another country because he wants to stay close to his family in Leeds.

Ann **4**_____ probably_____ (study) biology at college. She's

always wanted to be a scientist. In 20 years, she **5**_____

definitely _____ (earn) a good salary. She probably

**6**_____ (not live) in the United States because she's always

wanted to live in a foreign country.

Both Chris and Ann **7**_____ (bring up) big families. They

both want to have a lot of children.

**30** **Write the sentences in reported speech. Use said or said that with the person in parentheses.**

**1** "Children are the inventors of the future." (The researcher)

_____.

**2** "I think that we'll have nanopets in the future." (Ana)

_____.

**31** **Answer the questions. Use Yes, definitely, Yes, probably, No, probably not, or No, definitely not.**

**1** In your lifetime, do you think you'll be working with intelligent beings from outer space?

_____

**2** Do you think people will be living on other planets in the next century?

_____

# unit 5 IF I COULD FLY...

**1** Which super powers do these characters have? Match the characters with their super power. Write the numbers.

___ able to climb tall buildings          ___ has superhuman strength

___ runs faster than the wind             ___ disappears with the snap of a finger

___ saves the world from "bad guys"       ___ travels through time and space

**2** Look at 1 and answer the questions.

1  Which super power would make your life better?

_____

2  How would the super power improve your life?

_____

3  Who are your favorite superheroes? What powers do they have?

_____

**3** Match the beginning of the phrases with their endings. Then match the phrases with the pictures. Write the numbers under the pictures.

It's easy!
Now you see me!
Now you don't!

A ___    B ___    C ___    D ___

___ **1** run at          **a** invisible
___ **2** travel          **b** superhuman strength
___ **3** have            **c** lightning speed
___ **4** become          **d** through time

**4** Complete the sentences with the phrases in 3.

**1** I want to meet people who lived long ago. If I could have a super power, I would _____.

**2** I want to move around without people being able to see me. If I could have a super power, I would _____.

**3** I want to be able to get anywhere in a few seconds! If I could have a super power, I would _____.

**4** I want to be really strong so that I can pick up anything I want! If I could have a super power, I would _____.

**5** Complete the sentences. If you had these super powers, what would you do?

**1** If I could have superhuman strength, I would _____.

**2** If I could read minds, I would _____.

**3** If I could travel through time, I would _____.

Which super powers could help the police? How?

THINK BIG

_____
_____
_____

**6** Listen and read. Then circle **T** for true or **F** for false.

| | | | |
|---|---|---|---|
| **1** | Bulldog and Power Paws know each other. | T | F |
| **2** | Bulldog is happy to see Power Paws. | T | F |
| **3** | Bulldog isn't scared of Power Paws. | T | F |
| **4** | Bulldog knows that Power Paws is going to make him small. | T | F |
| **5** | Power Paws has special powers. | T | F |

**7** Answer the questions.

**1** What's Bulldog doing to Duck?

_____

**2** Why is Power Paws going to make Bulldog small?

_____

**3** Do you think Duck will take good care of Bulldog?

_____

**8** Listen and read. Then circle the correct answers.

**Girl:** Dad, do you think we'll ever be able to travel through time?

**Dad:** Wow, that's a hard one. A lot's possible today but I really don't see how time travel would be. Why do you ask?

**Girl:** I was just wondering. Imagine how much fun it would be if we could! If you could go back in time, where would you go?

**Dad:** Hmm. Let me think… Maybe I'd go back to see my great-grandparents who lived in London. My great-grandfather was a shoemaker there—have I ever told you that? I'm told he was quite a character. I'd love to talk to him. What would you do?

**Girl:** Me? Oh, I already know—that's easy. If I could travel through time, I'd go back to last night and review more. I don't feel ready for my math test this afternoon!

**1** The dad thinks the girl's question is ___ to answer.

   **a** easy          **b** not easy

**2** The girl ___ travel back in time.

   **a** wants to          **b** doesn't want to

**3** The girl ___ stories about her great-grandfather.

   **a** has heard          **b** hasn't heard

**4** The girl ___ hard for her math test.

   **a** studied          **b** didn't study

**9** Match the phrases with their meanings.

___ **1** That's a hard one.          **a** It means "to travel to a time in the past."

___ **2** go back in time          **b** It means "a funny, interesting, unique person" that people like.

___ **3** quite a character          **c** It means "I need a little time to think about my answer."

___ **4** Let me think.          **d** It means "That's a difficult question." You say this when the question isn't easy to answer.

**10** Complete the sentence. Use a phrase from 9.

The teacher asks you, "Who's your favorite superhero?" You need to think about your answer so you say _____ .

# Language in Action

| *if* clause | result clause |
|---|---|
| If I **were** you, | **I'd choose** something else. |
| If he **made** his bed every day, | his mom **would be** happy. |
| If she **could have** one super power, | she**'d breathe** underwater. |

**II** Complete the sentences with the words given.

1 (would, study, were) If I _____ you,
I _____ harder. You would get better grades.

2 (could, would, fly, visit) If she _____ ,
she _____ her aunt and uncle in Scotland all the time.

3 (could, would, run, win)  If the track team _____ at lightning
speed, it _____ all its competitions.

4 (would, be, did) If all the students _____ their homework all
the time, the teacher _____ happy.

5 (could, would, know, read) If I _____ my teacher's mind,
I _____ the answers to all her questions.

**I2** Read. Complete the speech bubbles with the words given. Use could and would.

I can't sing well. But if I _____
(sing) well, I _____ (join) a band.

My friends and I can't travel back in time. If
we _____ (travel) back in
time, we _____ (meet) our
favorite heroes in history.

My older brother can't drive yet. If he
_____ (drive), he
_____ (take) me and
my friends to the movies.

My friend can't be quiet in class. If she
_____ (be) quiet, our
teacher _____ (be) happier.

**I3** Complete the sentences about yourself.

1 If I could meet a famous person, I _____ .

2 _____ , I would be very happy.

| | |
|---|---|
| If you **didn't have to go** to school, what **would** you **do** every day? | If I **didn't have to go** to school, I **would stay** home and **listen** to music all day. |
| If you **could go** anywhere, where **would** you **go**? | If I **could go** anywhere, I**'d go** to Paris. |

**14** **Complete the questions. Unscramble the words.**

(you / would / go / where)

**1** If you could visit any country you wanted to, _____?

(would / which language / you / learn)

**2** If you could learn another language (not English), _____?

(you / be / would / which animal)

**3** If you could be any animal, _____?

(be / who / you / would)

**4** If you could be any superhero, _____?

(would / play / which instrument / you)

**5** If you could play any instrument, _____?

**15** **Match the questions in 14 with the answers below. Write the numbers. Then circle T for true or F for false.**

___ **1** I would be a wolf because wolves are really smart animals.  T  F

___ **2** I would visit Italy to see the works of art.  T  F

___ **3** I would learn Chinese.  T  F

___ **4** I would be Spider-Man because I think it would be fun to climb walls.  T  F

___ **5** I would play the piano.  T  F

**16** **Ask a friend or family member the questions in 14. Write his or her answers.**

**1** _____

**2** _____

**3** _____

**4** _____

**5** _____

**17** Read and circle.

1 a substance that can stick things together, like glue      **a** electrode    **b** adhesive

2 a movement or action to show your feelings      **a** activate    **b** gesture

3 a small wire or metal that sends electricity through something      **a** electrode    **b** adhesive

4 to make something start working      **a** visualize    **b** activate

5 continuing for a very long time      **a** endless    **b** skyscraper

6 to see a mental image of      **a** visualize    **b** activate

**18** Listen and read. Match the titles A–E with the paragraphs 1–5.

**A** Super sticky adhesive        **D** Inventive products

**B** Perfect memory        **E** Super computers

**C** What do you think?

## Super Power or Invention?

1 ☐ Some researchers have developed products that seem to give us super power-like abilities. One of these inventions is the super sticky adhesive that they created by studying geckos and their sticky feet. Another invention would allow us to use our minds to tell a computer what to do. A third invention is our ability to visualize a computer anywhere we want one—even on our hands. Let's imagine what our lives might be like if we could buy these products today.

2 ☐ In the morning, you wake up. Your bed is stuck on the wall so you climb down a ladder to get to the floor. There is space under your bed now to hang out with friends so you like that. After breakfast, you put on your super sticky shoes and hand pads. On your way to school, you activate them and you climb up a wall to your friend Timmy's bedroom window. He sees you. You both climb down the wall and start walking to school.

3 ☐ "Oh, no!" you suddenly say, "I forgot my homework!" You think, "Mom, please send my math homework to school." Your mom gets the message on her smartphone and texts back, "OK." You think, "Thanks, Mom!" Your mind is connected to your computer at home so you can send messages to it or to your parents' smartphones. Then your friend says, "I wonder what the reviews are for the new superhero movie?" He draws a box on your backpack and a computer appears. He goes to a movie review website and reads the latest reviews to you as you walk.

4 ☐ At school, you climb up the wall and hang your jacket on a hook. Your teacher gives you a quiz and tells you, "Don't draw computers anywhere. If you've studied, you'll know every answer." You didn't study much so you're thinking, "If I could see the book in my mind, I could look up the answers." Researchers haven't worked out how to give you perfect memory—but they're probably working on it.

5 ☐ Thus, if we had these three inventions today, the possibilities would be endless. Think of all the things you could do with super sticky adhesive. Also, what would you tell a computer to do with your mind? Think of the many uses this super power would have for you. Imagine being able to visualize a computer whenever you need one, too. Life with these inventions would be very different from now. You would be a real superhero! What do you think?

## 19 Read 18 again and circle T for true and F for false.

**1** Researchers created super sticky adhesive from studying geckos' tongues.  **T**   **F**

**2** One invention is the ability to control a computer with our minds.  **T**   **F**

**3** You could stick your bed to the wall with super sticky adhesive.  **T**   **F**

**4** A third invention is the super power ability to remember things perfectly.  **T**   **F**

**5** If we had these inventions, life would be very different for us today.  **T**   **F**

## 20 Find and circle six words from 17.

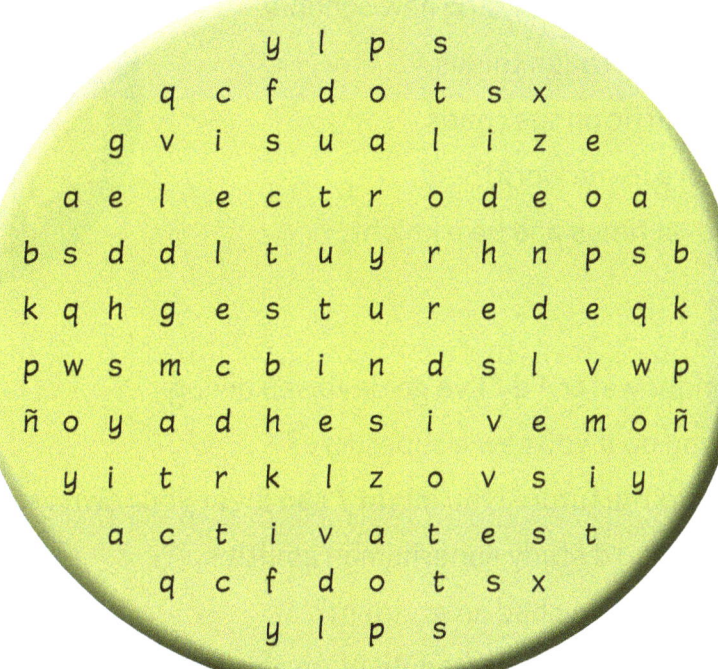

To "develop something" means that it takes a long time to make something work well. Which invention do you think took the longest time to create? Why?

_____

Pretend that you can draw computers anywhere and use them. Where would you use them? What would you do?

_____

# Grammar

**21** Read and match. Write the letters.

___ **1** If I were a superhero,

___ **2** What would you do if

___ **3** If I could travel back in time,

___ **4** Where would you go if

___ **5** If everybody walked to school,

___ **6** If I were the president,

**a** you could connect to a computer in your mind?

**b** I would spend more money on building new schools.

**c** I'd like to be able to see through things.

**d** there might be less traffic on the roads.

**e** you could go anywhere in the world?

**f** I'd go back to medieval times and be a knight.

**22** Read and circle.

**1** If I could breathe under water, **I'd / I've** go deep sea diving.

**2** What **may / would** you do if you saw a superhero?

**3** If you could travel into the future, you **might / can** meet your own grandchildren!

**4** If I **am / were** a scientist, I'd study superhuman abilities.

**5** What **could / can** you do if you had an accident?

**6** If I moved to another country, I **will / would** learn a new language.

**23** Unscramble and write.

1 invisible / what would / if you were / you do

_____

2 a good swimmer / I'd swim / if I were / across the channel

_____

3 if you could / where would / study anywhere / you study

_____

4 the bus / on time / they might catch / if they left

_____

**24** Complete the sentences with the correct form of the verb in parentheses. Use would where necessary.

1 If you _____ (can) invent something, what _____ (it / be)?

2 If I _____ (study) computer technology, I _____ (invent) something amazing one day!

3 What _____ (you / become) if you were good at math and science?

4 If I were you, I _____ (offer) to help more at home.

5 If you _____ (leave) now, you _____ (not be) late.

**25** Complete the sentences for you. Use If I were… or If I could.

1 _____ , I would donate money to scientific research.

2 _____ , I might meet more people and make new friends.

3 _____ , I would improve my English.

4 _____ , I would run very fast!

**26** Read and ✔.

1  a long, loose, sleeveless coat that fastens around your neck    **a** costume ☐    **b** cape ☐

2  clothes someone wears to look like someone or something else    **a** costume ☐    **b** cape ☐

3  something terrible that happens, which affects you for a long time    **a** trauma ☐    **b** accident ☐

4  by chance, not planned    **a** trauma ☐    **b** accidentally ☐

5  started in a particular place or time    **a** native ☐    **b** originated ☐

6  born in a particular country    **a** native ☐    **b** originated ☐

**27** 82 Listen and read. Write the names of the superheroes.

1  Human weapons cannot destroy this superhero. _____

2  Bolts of lightning are weapons of this superhero. _____

3  This superhero acts like a cat. _____

## Superhuman Superheroes!

Superheroes from around the world have unique abilities to help them protect people and destroy evil. Many superheroes have suffered a trauma and want to save people from the same thing that happened to them. Other superheroes got their super powers from something that happened to them accidentally. Many superheroes originated in the USA, but some countries have their own superheroes. Here are some examples:

Cat Girl Nuku Nuku is a native of Japan. She's a college student but when something terrible happens, she becomes a superhero! She can react quickly, just like a cat. She can smell, see, and hear very well because she has the senses of a cat. She also has superhuman strength.

Meteorix is from Mexico. He's at college, too, and his everyday name is Aldo. He also has superhuman strength and can throw bolts of lightning. When he has to protect himself, he covers himself with blue armor by swallowing a meteorite.

Darna is a native of the Philippines. Her everyday name is Narda and she's a student as well. Darna can fly and has superhuman strength and speed. She can't be destroyed by weapons that humans make. She can change back and forth between her two identities, Darna and Narda, by swallowing a stone and shouting the name of her other identity.

Superheroes are fun to read about but do you sometimes wish that they were real? If these superheroes were real, they would have a lot to do every day!

**28** Read **27** again and answer the questions.

1 Where did many superheroes originate? _____

2 Why can Nuku Nuku hear, see, and smell very well?

_____

3 Whose name is also Aldo? _____

4 Why does Meteorix cover himself with blue armor? _____

5 Where is Darna from? _____

6 How can Darna change identities?

_____

**29** Unscramble and write words from **27**. Then complete the sentences.

1 _____  liev      Many superheroes help to destroy _____.

2 _____  nseess    Cat Girl has super power _____.

3 _____  lbost     Meteroix can throw _____ of lightning.

4 _____  awenosp   Darna can't be destroyed by human _____.

**Read. Which superhero can help? Why?**

Some bank robbers are coming out of a bank. They have a very big weapon. They're running away!

_____

THINK
**BIG**

An evil person from space wants to steal all the gold and diamonds in the world. It's hard to find her because she's very tiny and can hide very easily.

_____

Some bad guys have thousands of fighters helping them. The bad guys want to destroy the government. The bad guys are attacking now!

_____

When you write a description of a character, describe everything about that character:

**1** name(s)          **2** appearance
**3** occupation       **4** super powers
**5** country of origin **6** family
**7** time period that he or she lives in:  **8** mission
      now, the future, the past

**30** Read the sentences and match them with the information in the box. Write the numbers. Be careful! What information is missing? Write the numbers.

___ Her everyday name is Diana but her superhero name is Wonder Woman.

___ She has superhuman strength and she's an excellent fighter. She has a rope that makes people tell the truth and an invisible jet.

___ She has a place near Greece in ancient times.

___ She has a lot of sisters.

Missing information: Numbers ___ ___ ___ ___

**31** Read the missing information from 30 below. Number it according to the information in the writing box.

___ lived in the past and lives in the present, too          ___ make villains honest
___ in many stories she's an officer in the army             ___ is tall / has long dark hair

**32** Write a description of Wonder Woman. Use the information in 30 and 31.

_____

_____

_____

_____

_____

_____

**33** Match the phrases to make sentences. Write the letters.

___ **1** What would you do if

___ **2** If you ran at lightning speed,

___ **3** If I could travel back in time,

___ **4** If you could fly anywhere,

**a** you'd be faster than a train.

**b** you could read people's minds?

**c** where would you go?

**d** I might see my grandfather as a boy.

**34** Complete the sentences with your own ideas.

**1** If _____ , I might know why you're angry with me.

**2** If _____ , I'd move your house closer to mine. Then I could see you more often.

**3** If you invented something to help other people, _____ ?

**4** What would you _____ ?

**35** Read. Circle the correct answers.

**1** If people ___ wings, they wouldn't drive cars.

   **a** have         **b** had

**2** If she had enough money, she ___ those silver earrings.

   **a** 'd buy       **b** buys

**3** You're really smart. If I ___ you, I'd try out for a TV quiz show.

   **a** were        **b** be

**4** If my older brother went to bed earlier, he ___ so tired every morning.

   **a** 's not going to be    **b** wouldn't be

**36** Answer the questions with your own ideas.

**1** If you found $20, what would you do with the money?

_____

**2** If you wrote a book, what would you write about?

_____

**3** If you owned a flying car, where would you go and why?

_____

# unit 6 THE COOLEST SCHOOL SUBJECTS

**1** Which school subjects do the pictures show? Write the numbers.

___ geography        ___ literature

___ history of art     ___ world history

___ science          ___ P.E.

___ music            ___ math

**2** If you could choose three subjects to add to your school schedule, what would they be? Mark (✔) or add your own ideas.

☐ computer science      ☐ government

☐ Chinese             ☐ chemistry

☐ orchestra          ☐ tennis

☐ theater             ☐ ecosystems and ecology

☐ _____     ☐ _____

**3** Unscramble the words. Use the words to complete the sentences.

**1** M Y C R O E A C D _____

The word _____ comes from a Greek word that means "power of the people." One of the first Western examples of this form of government was in Athens, in the fifth century BC.

**2** M A M L A M _____

The cheetah is the fastest _____ in the world. It can run about 100 meters in six seconds!

**3** P T N A L _____

The bladderwort is the deadliest meat-eating _____. It can kill an insect in less than a millisecond.

**4** G I Y R H W A L T P S _____

Shakespeare is one of the most famous _____ in English literature. He wrote approximately 40 plays in his lifetime, including comedies, tragedies, and historical plays.

**5** P E R M I B E U R N M _____ _____

The number 8 can be divided by 1 and 8 but it can also be divided by 2 and 4. As a result, it is not a _____ _____.

**4** Match these sentences with the subjects. Write the letters.

____ **1** I want to learn more about myths and legends.

____ **2** I love reading about democracies all over the world.

____ **3** We have a grammar test today.

____ **4** In today's lesson, we learned that blue whales are the largest mammals in the world!

____ **5** We're painting a mural on the wall today.

____ **6** I love playing soccer!

**a** P.E.

**b** English

**c** literature

**d** art

**e** social science

**f** science (biology)

**THINK BIG**

Is what you learn inside the classroom and what you learn outside the classroom equally important? Why/Why not?

_____

_____

**5** Listen and read. Then answer the questions.

# The Story of Daedalus and Icarus

Once upon a time, on the island of Crete, there was a man named Daedalus and his young son Icarus. They lived in the palace of King Minos. Daedalus was the smartest man in the palace. He was also one of the greatest inventors and architects of that time. He invented many things for the king, including an enormous type of maze called The Labyrinth. King Minos didn't want Daedalus to share the secrets of The Labyrinth with anyone so he put Daedalus and Icarus in prison. Daedalus was very unhappy. He had only one wish. He wanted to be free.

One day, Daedalus was watching the birds fly. He admired their beautiful, strong wings. Watching the birds gave him an idea. If he created wings for Icarus and himself, they could fly away and be free! So Daedalus created wings of feathers and wax and they put them on. Daedalus told Icarus, "Be careful! Don't fly too close to the water or you might fall into it! Don't fly too close to the sun or the wax will melt and you'll fall!" Icarus said that he would obey his father but when they started flying, Icarus became extremely excited. He flew in circles and went higher and higher. He loved the feeling of freedom and flying. His father called out to him, "Come back here! Don't go too close to the sun!" Icarus wanted to listen but the feeling of freedom was the best feeling in the world so he kept flying higher. The sun became hotter and hotter and began to melt the wax. Icarus started to fly lower but it was too late. Icarus's wings fell off and he fell into the sea and was lost.

**1** Why did King Minos put Daedalus and Icarus in prison?

_____

**2** Why did Daedalus want to escape?

_____

**3** Why did Icarus fly higher and higher?

_____

**4** What can we learn from this story?

_____

**5** The Icarian Sea was named after Icarus. Do you know any other places named after famous myths and legends? Write the names.

_____

**6** Listen and read. Then circle the correct answers.

**Julie:** I haven't reviewed for the math test yet, have you?

**Leo:** Not yet. Hey, <u>let's make a study group</u>!

**Julie:** That's the smartest idea you've had in a long time!

**Leo:** Ha! Ha! Very funny.

**Cathy:** Great idea! The only thing I remember about prime numbers is that they're larger than 1.

**Julie:** <u>Speaking of</u> prime numbers, do you know the most amazing thing about the numbers 3-7-9-0-0-9? Type them on a calculator and read them upside down. They spell GOOGLE.

**Leo:** <u>Seriously</u>? <u>Let me see</u>…. You're right! That's the coolest thing ever!

**379009**

**1** Why are Julie, Leo, and Cathy going to get together?

  **a** They're going to have fun.    **b** They're going to review for the math test.

**2** Does Cathy understand what prime numbers are?

  **a** Yes    **b** No

**3** Why is 379009 an amazing number?

  **a** It spells the word "GOOGLE" in numbers.  **b** It's the largest prime number.

**7** Look at **6**. Read the underlined expressions. How can you say them using other words? Match the expressions with the sentences. Write the letters.

  \_\_\_ **1** Let's make a study group.    **a** By the way, that reminds me of something.

  \_\_\_ **2** Speaking of…    **b** Really? I'm surprised.

  \_\_\_ **3** Seriously?    **c** Why don't we study together?

  \_\_\_ **4** Let me see.    **d** I want to try.

**8** Complete the dialogs with the expressions in **7**. Then listen and check your answers.

**A:** I was just chosen to be on a TV quiz program.

**B:** ¹_____? Congratulations!

**01134**

**A:** Yeah, they asked me what happens when you turn 01134 upside down. I said it spells "hello."

**B:** ²_____. Wow! You're right!

**A:** ³_____ numbers, ⁴_____ for the math test tomorrow.

**B:** Good idea!

China has **more** speakers of English **than** the USA.

I have **fewer** school subjects **than** my brother.

Teachers in Finland give **less** homework **than** teachers in the UK.

**9** Complete these facts about countries. Circle more, fewer, or less.

1 People in Germany spend 18 hours per week watching TV. People in the UK spend 28 hours. People in the UK spend **more / less** time watching TV than people in Germany.

2 According to the World Atlas, Europe has 47 countries and Asia has 44 countries. There are **more / less** countries in Europe than in Asia.

3 In Spain, there are approximately 19,000,000 males and 20,000,000 females. There are **less / fewer** males than females.

4 In Africa, people speak more than 2,000 languages. In North and South America, people speak almost 1,000 languages. People in Africa speak **more / less** languages than people in North and South America.

5 In the UK, the parrot is a **more / less** popular pet than a cat. People like cats better than parrots.

6 In India, 946 films are made per year. In the USA, 611 films are made per year. The USA makes **more / fewer** films per year than India.

**10** Answer the questions. Write complete sentences.

1 Do you watch more or fewer hours of TV per week than people in the UK?

_____

2 In your country, do you think a rabbit is a more or less popular pet than a cat?

_____

3 Do you think your country makes fewer or more films per year than the USA?

_____

4 Do you think your country has more or fewer people than Spain?

_____

5 In your class, are there more females or males?

_____

The Amazon rainforest has **the most** species of plants and animals on Earth.

Germany and Switzerland have **the fewest** pet dogs per capita.

Which country has **the least** amount of air pollution?

**11** Draw lines to connect the sentence parts.

1 A tree in Nevada, USA, is 4,800 years old. It's    the least    tourists of any city in Europe.

2 London has about 15 million tourists each year. It has    the longest    mammal in the world.

3 The kakapo parrot weighs 3.5 kilograms. It's    the oldest    amount of rain per year of all deserts.

4 It rarely rains in the Atacama Desert in Chile. It has    the lightest    parrot in the world.

5 Siberia has a very long railway. It has    the heaviest    railway in the world.

6 The bumblebee bat only weighs two grams. It's    the most    tree alive.

**12** Read the answers. Write the questions.

1 _____

The armadillo is one of the most endangered species in the Americas.

2 _____

The piranha has the sharpest teeth of all fish.

3 _____

The white millipede has the most legs of any animal. It has a total of 750 wiggling legs!

4 _____

The land mammal with the fewest teeth is the narwhal. It only has two large teeth.

**13** Write the words in the correct category. Then listen and check your answers.

| carnivore | herbivore | nectar |
|---|---|---|
| nutrient | protein | stem |

| Words that describe animals | Words that describe plants | Words that describe food |
|---|---|---|
|  |  |  |
|  |  |  |

**14** Listen and read. How tall can a pitcher plant grow?

# How to Take Care of a Pitcher Plant

Do you want to have a pet, but your parents won't let you? Perhaps your home is too small for a pet like a cat or a dog? Or perhaps your parents think that a pet hamster or bird may be too messy, or too noisy? If your parents won't allow pets in your home, you could try growing a pitcher plant. It could be your perfect "pet plant!" You can take care of it and feed it just like a pet. But be careful. At mealtimes, these plants get very hungry! So hungry they could eat a rat! Yes, this plant is the largest meat-eating plant in the world. In fact, pitcher plants have tall flowers and stems and can grow up to one meter tall!

Pitcher plants need lots of nutrients and protein. To be a good pitcher plant owner, you'll have to make sure that your plant gets lots of sunlight and water. These are important to keep your little carnivore happy and healthy. Water's especially important. It makes the top of the plant slippery so that insects can slip into the nectar. The plant is shaped like a cup, so insects are easily trapped in it. The sweet-smelling, sticky nectar helps the plant digest the food. The plant then uses chemicals to break down the proteins and nutrients in the food, and absorbs them.

Check your plant to make sure it's catching enough insects. Some days you'll have to feed it an extra insect or two if it looks hungry. Your pitcher plant will have the healthiest and happiest pet plant life of all if you love it and take good care of it.

**15** Read 14 again and answer the questions.

1 Why is the pitcher plant like a pet?

_____

2 What's unusual about the pitcher plant?

_____

3 How can you keep a pitcher plant healthy?

_____

4 How does the pitcher plant catch its food?

_____

**16** Complete the sentences with the words in the box.

absorb    carnivore    digest    nectar    nutrients

1 Most plants need water, sunlight and _____ to grow.
2 The pitcher plant is a _____ because it eats meat like insects and rats.
3 Most plants _____ nutrients from the soil.
4 Sunbirds use their long beaks to sip _____ from flowers.
5 We have chemicals in our stomachs to help our bodies _____ food.

THINK BIG

Would you like to own a pitcher plant? Would it make a good pet? Why / Why not?

_____

_____

_____

# Grammar

**17**  Read and circle.

1  We **have to / don't have to** be quiet in the library, so that we don't disturb others.

2  You **must / mustn't** arrive on time or else you will miss the show.

3  She **has to / doesn't have to** join the computer club if she doesn't want to!

4  They **must / mustn't** forget to collect their artwork before they go home.

5  Simon **has to / doesn't have to** study hard, so that he can pass his exams.

6  You **have to / don't have to** help at the bake sale, as there are enough helpers already.

**18**  Read and complete the classroom rules with must or mustn't.

1  You _____ be kind and polite to others.

2  You _____ be late for class.

3  You _____ call out or talk when others are speaking.

4  You _____ look after your belongings.

5  You _____ ask for help when you need it.

6  You _____ leave the classroom without telling the teacher.

**19**  Look and complete the sentences. Use have to / has to or don't have to / doesn't have to.

1  She _____ tidy her bedroom before she goes out. (✔)

2  We _____ buy tickets as we've already gotten them. (✘)

3  He_____ practice playing the piano every day. (✘)

4  They _____ eat all their vegetables at supper time. (✔)

5  I _____ drink plenty of water today as it's so hot. (✔)

6  These plants _____ be watered every day. If they have too much water, they will die. (✘)

**20** Unscramble and write the sentences.

**1** read a story / have to / to my class / I

_____

**2** dirty water / you / drink / mustn't

_____

**3** human brain / we / make a model / have to / of the

_____

**4** their parents / must tell / where / they / they're going

_____

**5** doesn't have to / summer camp / Michaela / go to

_____

**6** interrupt / is speaking / he / while someone / mustn't

_____

**21** Write 6 rules and suggestions for summer camp. Use must / mustn't or have to / don't have to.

**1** _____

**2** _____

**3** _____

**4** _____

**5** _____

**6** _____

**22** Read the words in the box and look at the chart. Then listen and write the words in the correct place.

Arabic zero (0)      calendar         chocolate          democracy          herbal remedies
myths                number system    Olympic Games      terraced farming

**The Greeks**
- Literature _____
- Sports _____
- Politics _____

**The Mayans**
- Astronomy _____
- Math _____

**The Aztecs**
- Math _____
- Food _____

**The Incas**
- Agriculture _____
- Medicine _____

**23** Listen and read. Which ancient civilization should you thank for things you have today?
Write **The Aztecs**, **The Incas**, or **The Greeks**.

# WHICH CIVILIZATION?

1 _____

This ancient civilization has had a very important influence on the modern world. For example, your favorite athletes can compete to be the best in the world at the Olympic Games, thanks to this ancient culture. When you get bored, you can read incredible stories about heroes, gods, and goddesses, too, as this culture has left us with an amazing legacy of literature.

2 _____

This ancient civilization gave us a type of farming that is still practiced today in many countries around the world. For example, the people in Thailand and Vietnam grow rice and other crops on hills using terraced farming. When you get ill, your mom or the doctor might give you herbal remedies to make you feel better. Many of these herbal remedies were also discovered by this ancient civilization.

3 _____

When you get hungry and want something sweet, you might enjoy eating a chocolate bar. You have this ancient civilization to thank for the cultivation of cacao, which is the main ingredient in chocolate. Mmmm... chocolate!

**24** Read 23 again and circle **T** for **true** or **F** for **false**.

1 At the Olympic Games, athletes compete to be the best in the world.     **T**     **F**

2 Stories about gods and goddesses come from ancient literature.     **T**     **F**

3 Thai and Vietnamese farmers grow their crops on flat land.     **T**     **F**

4 People may use herbal remedies when they are ill.     **T**     **F**

5 Cacao is not the main ingredient in chocolate.     **T**     **F**

**25** Complete the sentences with the words in the box.

> calendar     democracy     herbal remedies     myths     terraced farming

1 There are many ancient _____ and legends, which people still enjoy reading today.

2 _____ is a method used to grow crops on hills or mountains.

3 _____ is a form of government that is practiced in many countries in the world.

4 Our _____ consists of 365 days per year, which are divided into 12 months.

5 Many people believe that ancient _____ used to cure illnesses are better than modern medicine.

THINK BIG

**Think and write about one more thing for which you should thank an ancient civilization.**

_____

_____

A play tells a story. Both a play and a story have…

- Characters
- Important events
- An order of events

But a play is a special kind of story. It tells the story through dialogs and actors speaking those dialogs. The dialogs show what the people want, what they're thinking, and what's happening or has happened. The dialog is the only thing that tells us about the characters and events.

**26** **Read the story of Daedalus and Icarus in 5 again. Answer the questions.**

**1** How many characters are there in the story?

_____

**2** What are the names of the characters?

_____

**3** How would you describe each of the characters?

_____

_____

**4** There are three events mentioned in the story.

What happened first? _____

What happened second? _____

What happened in the end? _____

**5** What do these characters say, think, or wish in the story?

King Minos: _____

_____

Daedalus: _____

_____

Icarus: _____

_____

**27** **On a separate piece of paper, rewrite one of the events as a play. Tell the story of the event as a dialog between two of the characters. Use your notes in 26.**

**28**  **Read and match. Write the letters.**

___ **1** In English, we have to read aloud together

___ **2** For math, he mustn't forget

___ **3** In science class, they don't have to

___ **4** In history, I must do

**a** work in groups to do the experiment.

**b** my own research about ancient Greece.

**c** to bring his homework.

**d** a poem by Shakespeare.

**29**  **Read and complete the sentences with more or fewer.**

**1** A spider has eight legs. An ant has six legs.

The spider has _____ than an ant.

**2** I have two pets. My friend Alex has three pets.

I have _____ than Alex.

**3** London has about eight million people. Birmingham has almost one million people.

London has _____ than Birmingham.

**4** My pitcher plant eats four insects a day. Your pitcher plant eats six insects a day.

My pitcher plant eats _____ than yours.

**30**  **Complete the sentences. Use the least, the fewest, or the most and the underlined words.**

**1** Children in Finland don't do much homework.

They _____ of any European country.

**2** France has a lot of pet owners.

It _____ of any European country.

**3** Canada has a small number of mammals.

It _____ of any country in the world.

**4** Approximately 32 percent of families in the USA own dogs. That's more than any other country.

It _____ of any country in the world.

**THINK BIG**

1 **Look at Units 4, 5, and 6. Choose words from the units. Write them in the charts.**

### DREAMS FOR THE FUTURE

_____

_____

_____

_____

### SUPER POWERS

_____

_____

_____

_____

### SCHOOL INTERESTS

_____

_____

_____

_____

**2** Make a list of your superheroes – real or imaginary.

**3** Look at **2**. Choose one superhero and make some notes about your choice.

His/Her Dreams

_____

_____

_____

His/Her Powers

_____

_____

_____

His/Her Interests

_____

_____

_____

**4** Look at **1**, **2**, and **3**. Write a song about your superhero. Use some of these sentences in your song. Add your own sentences.

I'll save my best numbers for you.

If I could fly like Superman…

Pow! Bam! Slam! Kaboom!

Superhero, here I am.

I'll be living on the moon.

I've got my super power.

I'll be traveling through time soon.

# MYSTERIES!

**1** Match the pictures with the explanations of these unsolved mysteries. What do you think? Are these explanations possible? Circle Possible or Not Possible.

| | | |
|---|---|---|
| ___ Overnight, the wind creates unusual circles in farmer's fields. | **Possible** | **Not Possible** |
| ___ Giant pre-historic ape-like men still live in the Himalayas of Asia. | **Possible** | **Not Possible** |
| ___ Large, heavy rocks weighing up to 300 kilos move from place to place by themselves. | **Possible** | **Not Possible** |
| ___ The 246-page, 15th-century book of drawings and strange letters was written as a hoax to fool people and it doesn't really mean anything. | **Possible** | **Not Possible** |
| ___ Aliens from outer space created perfectly round sculptures in Costa Rica. | **Possible** | **Not Possible** |

**2** Complete the dialogs. Then listen and check your answers.

> explanation    Great Pyramids    northern lights    proof
> scientific       theories           unsolved

**A:** Have you ever heard of the ¹_____?

**B:** Yes, I think so. They're those bright, colorful lights in the night sky. They're caused by light reflecting off the ice caps in the Arctic.

**A:** No, that was just a theory. Now there's ²_____

³_____ . Gases in the air cause these nighttime fireworks.

**A:** The ⁴_____ in Egypt are incredible, aren't they?

**B:** They certainly are. Does anyone have an ⁵_____ of how they were built?

**A:** Well, some scientists have ⁶_____ about it but the

mystery is still ⁷_____ .

**3** Read the sentences about the places in 2. Circle T for true or F for false. Correct the false sentences.

**1** The Great Pyramids are an unsolved mystery but scientists have some theories about them.    T    F

_____

**2** There is scientific proof about how the Great Pyramids were built.    T    F

_____

**3** The northern lights appear in the night sky over Egypt.    T    F

_____

Do you think that most mysteries can be explained by science? Why/Why not?

_____

**Listen and read. Then answer the questions.**

# The Voynich Manuscript

The Voynich manuscript, written in the 15th century in Western Europe, is beautiful to look at. The pages of this "book" are full of colorful, lovely drawings of plants and astronomical objects, like suns and moons. The handwriting that surrounds the drawings appears to describe herbal remedies from plants. You can imagine that the author was a doctor or a scientist. But if you look more closely, you'll notice two very strange things: The words aren't in any known language and the plants don't exist. That's incredible, isn't it?

Scientists have studied the Voynich manuscript for years and have tried to understand the meaning of the words and the strange drawings. The words do follow some "rules" of a language or even two languages but scientists still cannot work out what the language is. And they don't know where the author learned about the strange plants. An early theory was that the writer used an artificial language. Another theory was that the whole thing was a hoax. But why would someone spend so much time on a manuscript and work so hard if it was just a prank?

Today, a group of scientists from around the world are working together to create a machine that will help them finally crack the code. What do you think? Will a computer be able to help them understand the information that the 15th-century writer so beautifully and carefully put into this manuscript?

### COMMENTS (2)

*Savvy Sam*

This is fascinating! What theories do scientists have about the plants? Could the plants be extinct species? They're amazing!

*Georgina*

I agree with Savvy Sam. The plants are amazing. I wonder if the plants look different because they're ancient? Plants could change over time, couldn't they? I hope scientists crack the code soon. Maybe the manuscript contains the cure for today's diseases. You never know!

1  How old is the Voynich manuscript?

_____

2  What's strange about the Voynich manuscript?

_____

**5** Listen and read. Then circle **T** for true or **F** for false.

**Tony:** I got you <u>hooked on</u> *Kryptos*, didn't I?

**Gerald:** You really did! I found lots of <u>cool stuff</u> about *Kryptos* online. Did you know that the creator of the codes has given more clues recently?

**Tony:** Seriously? What are the new clues?

**Gerald:** He gave six letters out of the 97 in the last phrase.

**Tony:** I bet the decoders got excited, didn't they?

**Gerald:** <u>Absolutely</u>. On the sculpture, the letters are NYPVTT. When decoded, the letters read BERLIN.

**Tony:** I can't imagine being a code breaker, can you? I wouldn't be able to sleep because I'd be thinking about it all the time.

**Gerald:** That's exactly what's happening. Lots of people are obsessed with cracking the code, and that's all they can think about every day.

**Tony:** <u>That's ridiculous</u>.

| | | |
|---|---|---|
| **1** Gerald is really interested in Kryptos. | T | F |
| **2** Gerald found out about Kryptos before Tony. | T | F |
| **3** Tony knew about the new clues that the creator gave out. | T | F |
| **4** Tony thinks a code breaker probably doesn't sleep much. | T | F |

**6** Match the expressions from **5** with the sentences. Write the letter.

___ **1** I'm hooked on it.

___ **2** Cool stuff.

___ **3** Absolutely.

___ **4** That's ridiculous.

**a** I agree with you completely.

**b** That's crazy. It's unreasonable.

**c** I'm obsessed with it.

**d** Interesting things.

**7** Complete the dialogs with the expressions in **6**. Then listen and check.

**1 A:** Jennifer's always reading.

**B:** I know. She's _____ historical mysteries. She reads all day, every day!

**A:** Really? _____.

**2 A:** There's a craft fair on Saturday. Let's go. They always have such _____, don't they?

**B:** _____. I could buy everything. Great idea!

# Language in Action

| AFFIRMATIVE STATEMENTS | NEGATIVE TAGS | NEGATIVE STATEMENTS | POSITIVE TAGS |
|---|---|---|---|
| The geoglyphs **are** in Peru, Experts **have** explained them, We **solved** the mystery, | **aren't** they? **haven't** they? **didn't** we? | Atlantis **isn't** real, Scientists **haven't** found it, It **didn't** make sense, | **is** it? **have** they? **did** it? |

**8** Complete the sentences with the correct question tags.

1 The Voynich manuscript is a mystery, _____?

2 The plants in the manuscript aren't real species, _____?

3 Scientists can't work out the language in the manuscript, _____?

4 The pictures of the plants are beautiful, _____?

5 The manuscript isn't a hoax, _____?

6 People can find a lot of information about the Voynich manuscript online, _____?

**9** Complete the sentences using question tags.

1 Scientists haven't found an explanation for the crop circles in England, _____?

2 The crop circles have perfect geometric patterns, _____?

3 The crop circle appeared in that field overnight, _____?

4 Proof for the theory that aliens created crop circles doesn't exist, _____?

**10** Unscramble the sentences. Write question tags.

1 don't / some people / in the Bermuda Triangle / do / believe / they

_____

2 don't / a mysterious / people / phenomenon / love / they

_____

3 didn't / the Nazca Lines / learned / we / a lot about / my classmates and I

_____

4 didn't / a theory for the Sailing Stones / did / scientists / have / for a long time / they

_____

5 seem / the city of Atlantis / does / doesn't /real / it

_____

**11** Zack is writing a play about Atlantis. Help him complete the play. Use the question tags in the box.

> didn't they?     don't we?     do they?
> isn't it?     wasn't he?     were they?

**Tabitha:** Well, here we are in the city of Atlantis! Wow! It's really cool,
¹ _____

**Brian:** Yeah. Look at that huge water fountain! It's beautiful!

**Tabitha:** We look a little funny wearing jeans and T-shirts,
² _____

**Brian:** I told you that we'd look strange. Look at that wall. It's covered in gold and silver!

**Tabitha:** All the walls are covered in metals. Scientists don't really know why this place disappeared, ³ _____

**Brian:** No, but Plato seemed to know. He said that the gods destroyed Atlantis.

**Tabitha:** Right. The people weren't good, ⁴ _____ So the gods destroyed the city with an earthquake and giant waves, ⁵ _____

**Brian:** That's right. Hey, look at that hill. Why is there a hill in the middle of the city?

**Tabitha:** Look at the top.

**Brian:** Oh, that's right. That's the temple of Poseidon. He was a very scary god,
⁶ _____

**Tabitha:** Absolutely. It's great to travel back in time.

**12** Listen and read. Then complete the diagram with the words in the box.

> atom (3)    nitrogen (2)    oxygen    solar winds

## What Causes the Aurora Borealis?

The aurora borealis or "Northern Lights," whose colors light up the night sky, is one of the most beautiful phenomena on Earth. It is also one of the most mystifying since the display of shimmering colors, lines, and shapes is different every time it appears. In the past, there were various theories explaining the appearance of this beautiful swirling display. For example, long ago in Finland, people thought the lights came from a mystical fox flashing its tail in the sky. The Algonquin tribe in Canada thought that the lights came from the god that created them. They believed that after the god finished, he went up north to live. The god showed his love for his people by making large spectacular fires that they could see and enjoy. Over the years, different myths have been told to explain this extraordinary phenomenon that may be best seen during the winter months in the Arctic. The aurora borealis continues to inspire writers, artists, and musicians today.

However, in 2008, scientists developed a theory that everyone could agree on. The spectacular lights were caused by the solar wind blowing around ions, atoms, gases, and other things in the atmosphere and making them collide. When they collide, they produce the colorful displays of light. So, how does it actually happen? The exact process is complicated but perhaps this simple diagram can help.

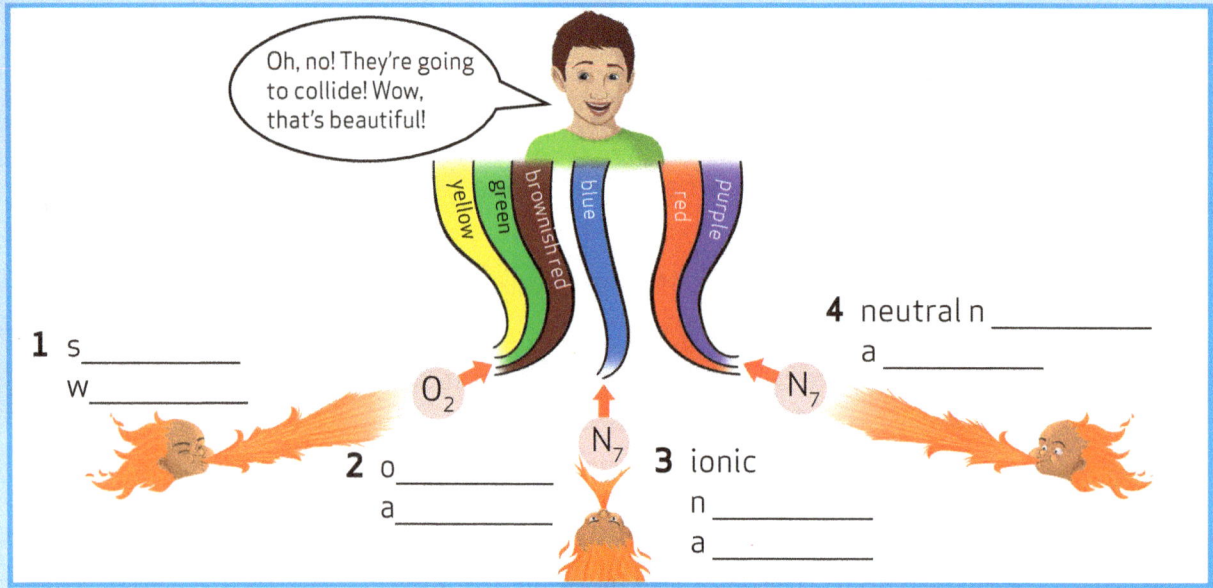

The hot solar winds from the sun are blowing oxygen and nitrogen atoms around. There are two kinds of nitrogen atoms—the neutral and the ionic. The atoms are full of energy. When they collide, they give off colors. Oxygen produces a yellow-green to brownish red color. The neutral nitrogen atoms produce purple and red colors. The ionic nitrogen atoms produce blue colors.

This is a simple explanation of how the aurora borealis is formed. It's good to understand the science behind the phenomenon, but the myths are fun to know, too, aren't they?

**13** Read 12 again and choose the correct answers.

**1** Each time the aurora borealis appears, it looks ___.

    **a** different                   **b** the same

**2** In the past, people in Finland thought the aurora borealis was a mystical ___ in the sky.

    **a** fire                          **b** fox

**3** Scientists discovered that the Northern Lights were caused by ___ blowing around gases in the atmosphere.

    **a** strong winds            **b** solar winds

**4** When neutral nitrogen atoms collide, they produce ___.

    **a** red and purple colors       **b** a blue color

**14** Complete the sentences using the words in the box.

> collide    energy    phenomena    shimmering    spectacular

**1** Many people believe that sand storms are one of the most amazing _____ in the natural world.

**2** The dancer wore a beautiful dress made of _____ colors that shone in the light.

**3** After the thunderstorm, there was a _____ rainbow that brightened the sky.

**4** When two cars _____ there can be a serious accident.

**5** Athletes have to make sure they eat plenty of foods that give them enough _____ to perform well.

THINK BIG

Can you think of any other natural phenomena? Is there a myth to explain their existence?

_____

_____

_____

_____

# Grammar

**15** Match. Write the letters.

___ **1** half-          **a** tempered

___ **2** ten-           **b** known

___ **3** good-          **c** year-old

___ **4** bad-           **d** sleeved

___ **5** well-          **e** asleep

___ **6** long-          **f** looking

**16** Complete the sentences using the words in the box.

> expensive-looking    five-kilometer    old-fashioned    ten-dollar    world-famous

**1** My grandfather drives an _____ car, which he bought 20 years ago.

**2** We went for a _____ walk along the beach yesterday.

**3** His mother gave him a _____ bill to spend at the amusement park.

**4** The Coliseum is a _____ site in Rome.

**5** He has a really _____ cell phone, which must have cost a lot of money.

**17** Unscramble and write the words.

**1** _____    lafh-kawea

**2** _____    dogo-mtereepd

**3** _____    wto-lokitmeer

**4** _____    nte-raye-ldo

**18** **Read and circle.**

1 **A**: I don't feel like eating right now.　　**B**: So do I. / Neither do I.

2 **A**: We enjoy learning about unsolved mysteries.　　**B**: So do we. / Neither do we.

3 **A**: Angelo doesn't have a cell phone.　　**B**: So does Daphne. / Neither does Daphne.

4 **A**: Her teacher is really kind.　　**B**: So is his. / Neither is his.

5 **A**: He's never seen a shooting star.　　**B**: So has she. / Neither has she.

6 **A**: They're going on holiday to Brazil.　　**B**: So am I. / Neither am I.

**19** **Read and complete the answers using the words in the box.**

> are　　does　　have　　is

1 I've never seen the aurora borealis.　　Neither _____ I.

2 My father is coming to watch us today.　　So _____ mine.

3 We are learning about the Great Pyramids.　　So _____ we.

4 She doesn't know how to play that game.　　Neither _____ he.

**20** **Write your own sentences for these positive and negative agreements.**

1 **A**: _____ **B**: So do I.

2 **A**: _____ **B**: Neither has she.

3 **A**: _____ **B**: So is mine.

4 **A**: _____ **B**: Neither was his.

5 **A**: _____ **B**: So can we.

**21** Complete the sentences using the words in the box.

> artifact  evidence  legend  mystery  sighting

1 There is a local _____ about an enormous water snake that lives at the bottom of the river.

2 After the fishermen told everyone about their _____ of the sea monster, people rushed onto the beach to try to see it.

3 He found an interesting _____ from the Stone Age, while exploring in the cave.

4 Scientists are trying to collect DNA _____ that will prove that the yeti exists.

5 Crop circles are an unsolved _____ .

 117

**22** Listen and read. What color is a yeti's fur?

# Huge, Hairy Ape-like Creatures: Real or Hoax?

All around the world, there are stories of strange sightings, amazing phenomena, and incredible artifacts. There are myths and legends to explain them, and some have inspired writers, poets, and artists. Researchers have tried to find scientific evidence to explain these mysteries in an attempt to discover whether they are real or just a hoax. The yeti (also known as the abominable snowman, Bigfoot, or Sasquatch) is one such example.

Huge, hairy, ape-like creatures have been the "stars" of at least ten films in Hollywood over the years. In some films, the creature is friendly and huggable like a teddy bear. In other films, it's a terrifying beast that wants to destroy everyone and everything. In real life, this creature has several names, depending on the region of the world in which it's seen. In the United States and Canada, the creature is called Bigfoot or Sasquatch. In the Himalayan regions of Asia, it's called the yeti or the abominable snowman. The color of the fur may be different (the yeti usually has white fur and Bigfoot has dark brown or black), but they both appear to be up to 2.7 meters tall and weigh from 300 to 400 kilos. Their feet can be as large as 43 centimeters long. But are these creatures real?

For years, scientists have thought that these creatures were a hoax, but to this day people continue to claim they've seen them. In 2012, there were many sightings in the United States. One person posted his video on YouTube and the video was seen more than 2 million times.

A theory of some scientists is that the creature is a Gigantopithecus, a giant, ape-like species that scientists thought was extinct. There hasn't been any proof for this theory, but the mystery may soon be solved. Scientists think they have some DNA samples from sightings. If the tests are positive, then the mystery creatures will finally become part of the amazing, fascinating world of science. If they're negative, these creatures will be part of myths and legends. Whatever the result, it seems clear that these creatures will continue to appear in real-life sightings, in stories, and in movies. Why? Because we love mystery and fantasy and we love to be surprised–at times, even frightened!–by the world around us.

**23**  Read 22 again and answer the questions.

1   Where is the abominable snowman called "Sasquatch"?

_____

2   How tall is the abominable snowman?

_____

3   How large are its feet?

_____

4   When and where were there many sightings of "Bigfoot"?

_____

5   What is a Gigantopithecus?

_____

6   What will prove that the yeti exists?

_____

**24**  Read and ✔.

1   an occasion when someone sees something rare or unusual
    **a** region ☐                    **b** sighting ☐

2   things that show something is real or true
    **a** evidence ☐                  **b** samples ☐

3   something someone does to trick or deceive people
    **a** hoax ☐                      **b** myth ☐

4   a small example of something that shows what the rest is like
    **a** proof ☐                     **b** sample ☐

5   an object from the past
    **a** artifact ☐                  **b** evidence ☐

THINK BIG  Scientists think that the yeti and Bigfoot are the same creature. Why do you think they look different in different regions of the world?

_____

_____

One purpose for writing is to explain something. When you write a cause-and-effect paragraph, you explain *why* something happens.

- Why something happens is called a **cause**.
- The thing that happens is called an **effect**.

For example, the aurora borealis is a beautiful display of lights. The beautiful lights are an effect. Why do the lights happen? That's the cause.

**25** Read the paragraph. <u>Underline</u> the causes. (Circle) the effects.

The aurora borealis is a brilliant light show. Colored bands of light paint the night sky in certain parts of the world. What makes this happen? Solar winds interact with the upper part of the atmosphere, causing atoms of oxygen and nitrogen to become changed. As the atoms return to their normal state, they give off colors.

**26** Write a cause-and-effect paragraph about something that's happened to you or something you've read about in your science lessons. Use the chart below to organize your ideas.

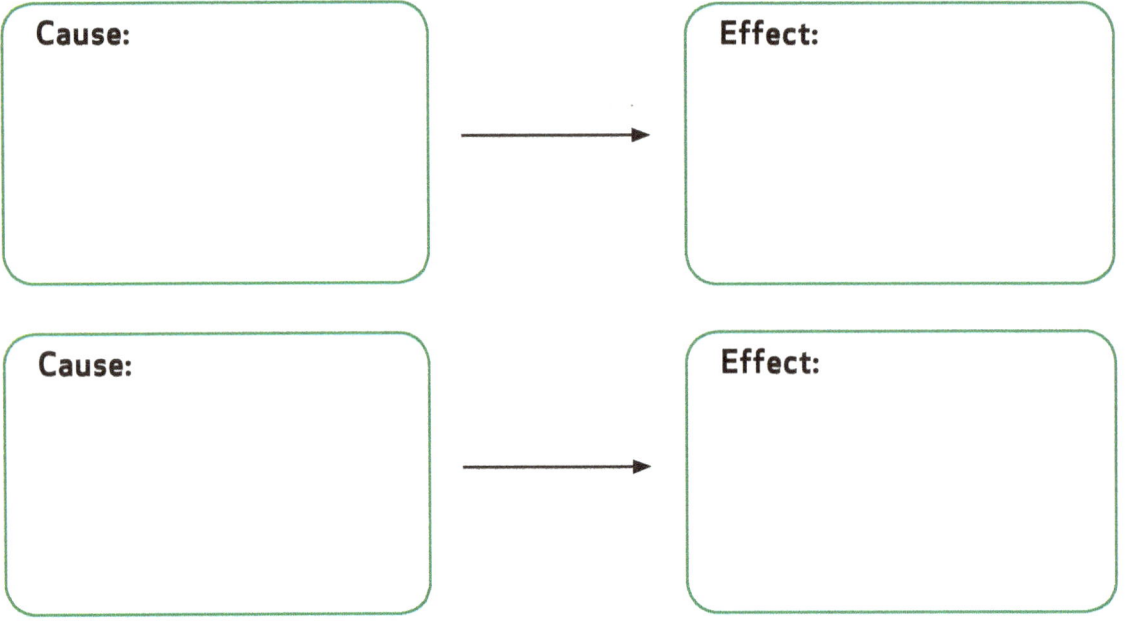

| Cause: | → | Effect: |

| Cause: | → | Effect: |

 **THINK BIG** If you could ask a scientist any question about why something happens, what would you ask?

_____

**27** Complete the sentences. Circle the answers.

1 There is no ___ for planes and boats disappearing in the Bermuda Triangle.

  **a** explanation          **b** phenomenon

2 Scientists know how the Sailing Stones move. That mystery is ___.

  **a** solved          **b** unsolved

3 Scientists think that crop circles are a hoax. This is a ___.

  **a** proof          **b** theory

4 Code breakers won't stop trying to crack the code until they have ___ proof that the Voynich manuscript really is a hoax.

  **a** solved          **b** scientific

**28** Correct the question tags.

1 The aurora borealis is a phenomenon in the northern hemisphere, is it?

  _____

2 The yeti lives in the Himalayas in Asia, isn't it?

  _____

3 There's proof that the Sailing Stones are real, aren't there?

  _____

4 The man who designed Kryptos wanted to challenge code breakers, didn't they?

  _____

5 Kryptos isn't a video game, isn't it?

  _____

**29** Complete the dialogs. Use question tags. Use the information you have learned about mysteries.

**A:** _____?

**B:** Neither have I. But I would love to know more about this mystery!

**A:** _____?

**B:** So do I. I'm very interested in learning more about this phenomenon.

# unit 8 WHY IS IT FAMOUS?

**1** Do you recognize these places? Match the descriptions with the pictures. Write the numbers. Why are these places famous? What do you think? Circle A for architecture, B for natural beauty, or C for mystery. You can circle more than one.

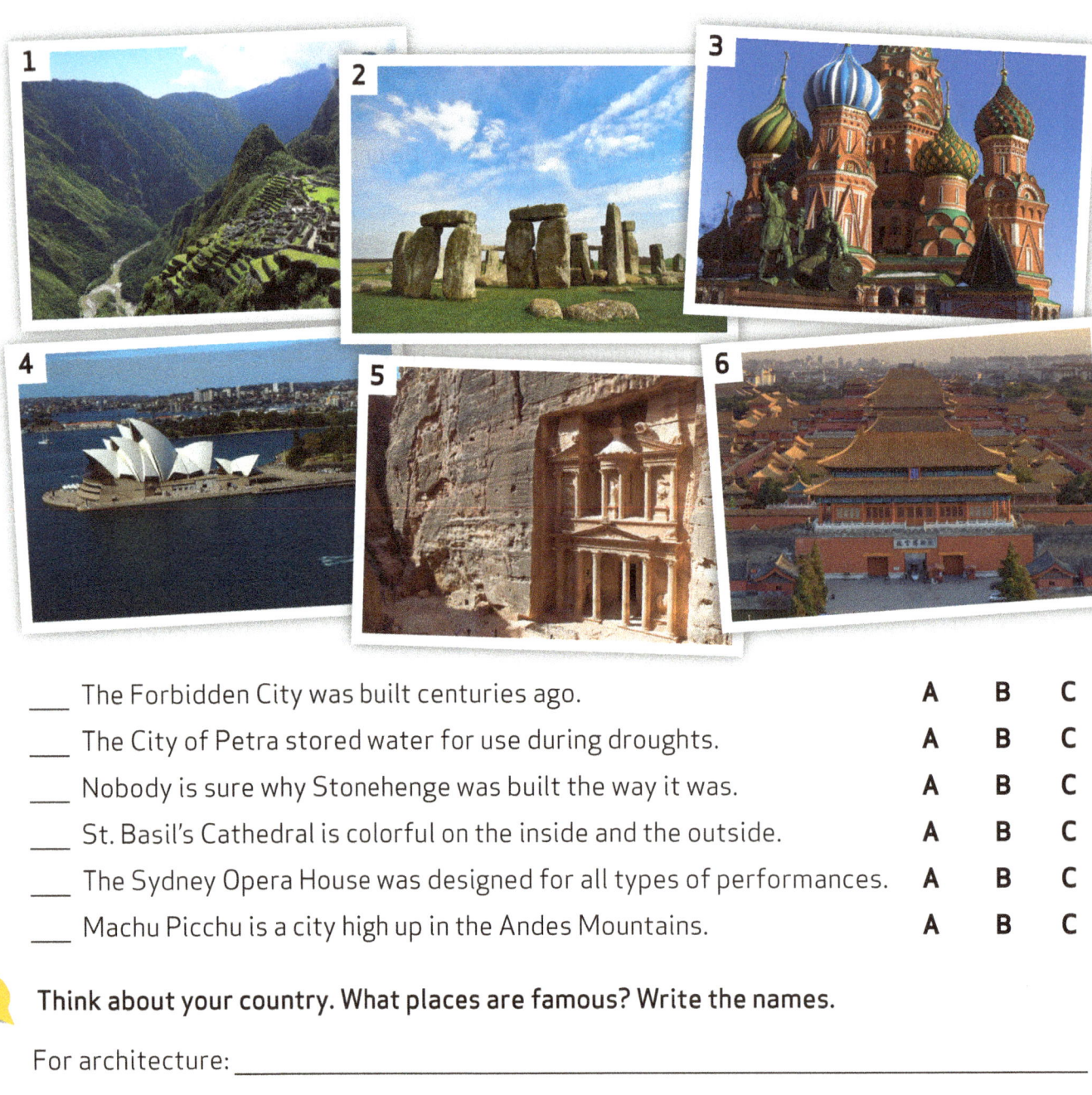

| | | A | B | C |
|---|---|---|---|---|
| ___ The Forbidden City was built centuries ago. | | A | B | C |
| ___ The City of Petra stored water for use during droughts. | | A | B | C |
| ___ Nobody is sure why Stonehenge was built the way it was. | | A | B | C |
| ___ St. Basil's Cathedral is colorful on the inside and the outside. | | A | B | C |
| ___ The Sydney Opera House was designed for all types of performances. | | A | B | C |
| ___ Machu Picchu is a city high up in the Andes Mountains. | | A | B | C |

**2** Think about your country. What places are famous? Write the names.

For architecture: _____

For natural beauty: _____

For mystery: _____

 **3** Listen and label the pictures with the words from the box.

mausoleum     monument     pyramid
statue     temple     tower

1 _____

2 _____

3 _____

4 _____

5 _____

6 _____

 **4** Answer the questions.

1 Look at **3**. If your class could travel to one of the places or structures, which one would you like to see?

_____

2 Have you ever visited a historic place like those pictured? What do you remember most about that place?

_____

_____

THINK
BIG

Does a landmark have to be old to be famous? Why/Why not?

_____

_____

**5** Listen and read. Then answer the questions.

# The Forbidden City

In the middle of Beijing, China, is the magnificent Forbidden City. Although now a museum and officially renamed the Palace Museum, or "Gugong" in Chinese, the Forbidden City was built in the early 1400s by Emperor Yongle as his imperial home. With 90 palaces and over 900 buildings, the Forbidden City was home to 24 Chinese emperors of the Ming and Qing dynasty for almost 500 years.

The Forbidden City is protected by a moat and a wall that is almost eight meters high. There is an inner court with buildings and rooms for the emperor and his family and an outer court with halls and gardens where the emperor did his work and entertained guests. Only people invited by the emperor were allowed into the palace. All others were forbidden to enter.

In front of the main gate, there is a pair of bronze lions. The male lion is holding a globe, symbolizing the power of the emperor. The female lion has a cub. She symbolizes the health and happiness of the emperor's family.

The colors yellow and red appear everywhere. Roofs of the buildings and bricks of the floor are yellow. Yellow symbolized the royal family and its supreme importance to the world. Doors, windows, pillars, and walls were often red. Red symbolized happiness and celebration.

Today, people come from all over the world to see the thousands of items in the Palace Museum; paintings, ceramics, jade pieces, clocks, jewelry, and sculptures all give us a glimpse of history. In 1987, the United Nations Educational, Scientific, and Cultural Organization (UNESCO) included the Forbidden City on its World Heritage List for its incredible architectural beauty and wealth of cultural artifacts.

**1** When was the Forbidden City built? Why was it built?

_____

**2** Why do you think the emperor's palace was called the Forbidden City?

_____

**3** There are statues of lions in front of the main gate. If you lived in a place like the Forbidden City, what animal statues would you have in front of your main gate? Why?

_____

**4** The colors red and yellow appear everywhere in the Forbidden City. If you lived in a place like the Forbidden City, what two colors would you use? What would they symbolize?

_____

**6** Listen and read. Then answer the question.

**Tania:** Hi, Eric! You're from Australia, aren't you?

**Eric:** Yes, I was born in Sydney. Why?

**Tania:** Well, I have to give a presentation in my art class. What do you know about the Sydney Opera House?

**Eric:** Quite a lot, actually. Did you know that the Opera House is <u>known for</u> its design?

**Tania:** Hmm. <u>That makes sense</u>. I've seen pictures and it's amazing, isn't it?

**Eric:** Yeah, it's a <u>work of art</u>! I don't know who designed it but I do know where the person was from. A design contest <u>was held</u> sometime in the 1950s and the person who won was from Denmark.

**Tania:** Really? You know, it looks like a big boat, doesn't it?

**Eric:** Yeah, I've heard other people say the same thing. It's amazing!

**Tania:** Thanks, Eric. You've given me a good start.

**Do Tania and Eric like the design of the Opera House? How do you know?**

_____

**7** Look at 6. Read the underlined expressions. How can you say them in other words? Match the expressions. Write the letter.

___ **1** known for

___ **2** That makes sense.

___ **3** work of art

___ **4** was held

**a** happened or took place

**b** painting, sculpture, or object that is skillfully made

**c** famous for

**d** That's logical. It's easy to understand.

**8** Complete the dialogs using the expressions in 7. Then listen and check.

**1 A:** My family is going to the city of Cambridge this weekend.

**B:** Really? I've heard of it but I don't know much about it.

**A:** It's _____ its architecture and its university, of course. You should go!

**2 A:** How was your holiday in Paris?

**B:** Great! We saw the Eiffel Tower. It's a phenomenal _____!

**3 A:** I'm doing research on Machu Picchu since we're going there on our next vacation.

**B:** _____.

# Language in Action

| Active | Passive |
|---|---|
| Archaeologists discovered Machu Picchu in 1911. | Machu Picchu **was discovered** in 1911 (by archaeologists). |

**9** Complete the sentences with the passive form of the verb in parenthesis and is/are.

1 The Galapagos Islands _____ (know) for their unique variety of animal and plant species.

2 The Forbidden City _____ (fill) with beautiful paintings and artifacts.

3 The Taj Mahal _____ (make) of marble.

4 The walls of the Taj Mahal _____ (decorate) with many floral designs.

5 The inside walls of St. Basil's Cathedral _____ (paint) every few years.

6 The Sydney Opera House _____ (locate) in Australia.

**10** Next to each sentence, write A for active or P for passive.

___ 1 Easter Island was discovered by Dutch explorers in 1722.

___ 2 It's still not known why the Moai statues on Easter Island were created.

___ 3 Trees were probably used to move the statues on Easter Island.

___ 4 Ivan the Terrible built St. Basil's Cathedral in Moscow in the mid-16th century.

___ 5 The city of Petra was constructed sometime around the 4th century BC.

___ 6 A Danish architect designed the Sydney Opera House.

**11** Write sentences with the passive form of the verbs in parentheses.

1 (call) El Castillo / the Pyramid at Kukulcán

_____

2 (rebuild) some of the stones of Stonehenge / in the early 20th century

_____

3 (give) The Statue of Liberty / to the United States as a gift

_____

> Leonardo da Vinci is the famous artist and inventor **who painted** the Mona Lisa.
> The Eiffel Tower is a landmark **that has become** the symbol of Paris, France.

**12** Write who or that.

1 The Galapagos Islands are named after the huge tortoises _____ are native to the island.

2 Charles Darwin studied the plants and animals _____ lived on the Galapagos Islands in the early 1800s.

3 It was Charles Darwin _____ made the Islands famous.

4 The tortoises and lizards aren't afraid of the visitors _____ come to see them.

5 The animal _____ is the best known of all is the Galapagos Tortoise.

**13** Match the sentences. Write the letters.

___ 1 Machu Picchu is an ancient city.

___ 2 Many tourists get to Machu Picchu by walking on paths.

___ 3 Scientists don't know much about the Incas.

___ 4 Scientists know about the Spanish conquerors.

a They invaded the city in the 1500s.

b The city was built high in the Andes Mountains.

c The Incas lived in Machu Picchu long ago.

d The paths lead to the ancient city.

**14** Look at 13. Rewrite the matched sentences as one sentence. Use who or that.

1 _____

2 _____

3 _____

4 _____

**15** Read and circle the correct answers.

**1**  Someone who studies the remains left by people living long ago.

  **a** archaeologist      **b** scientist

**2**  A collection of valuable things such as gold, silver, and jewels.

  **a** remains      **b** treasure

**3**  To make a hole in the ground.

  **a** bury      **b** dig

**4**  To dig in the ground with the aim of finding ancient objects.

  **a** excavate      **b** carve

**5**  An object from the past, such as a tool or a weapon.

  **a** treasure      **b** artifact

**16**  Listen and read. Where was the farmer who lost his hammer?

## ACCIDENTAL DISCOVERIES

Do you ever wonder what the world around you looked like hundreds or even thousands of years ago? What do you know about the people that used to live where you live now? Although we can learn about history from visiting museums, reading books, and watching movies, we can uncover much of the past from discovering buried artifacts and even treasure in the ground beneath us.

There were probably children just like you who played in the places that you play in today. Below your feet there could be artifacts or even treasures from those times and you could discover them—even by accident. Not all discoveries are made by archaeologists, who may spend years researching ancient places. Some discoveries are made accidentally by people just like you.

One important accidental discovery occurred in 1992, in England. A farmer was working in the fields when he lost his hammer. He asked a neighbor to help him find it. His neighbor had a metal detector. The first thing the metal detector found was a silver spoon. Then it found some jewelry and gold coins. The surprised farmers asked for the help of archaeologists. When the archaeologists excavated, they were shocked to discover a large box with over 14,000 Roman gold and silver coins inside. They believed that the treasure came from the 4th and 5th centuries AD. The archaeologists found other artifacts as well, including the farmer's hammer. The artifacts were sold to museums and the farmers received 2.5 million pounds as payment! Now, wasn't this an amazing accidental discovery?

In another accidental discovery, workers in Wyoming, in the United States, were digging up land to make a football field. They discovered artifacts from an ancient village that existed as long ago as the 1st century AD. The artifacts included objects used in people's homes and in the fields, as well as coins and other treasures.

Do you think the past is just waiting for you to uncover it? It may be. So, the next time you walk out of your door, look carefully at the world around you. You never know what you might find!

**17** Read 16 again and answer the questions.

**1** What did the farmer discover?

_____

**2** What was he using when he made his discovery?

_____

**3** What did archaeologists believe?

_____

**4** What accidental discovery was made in Wyoming?

_____

**18** Complete the sentences using the words in the box.

> accidental    discovery    existed    hammer    metal detector

**1** The workman used a _____ and some nails to fix the broken door.

**2** Finding the beautiful necklace in the grass was _____ , as we weren't looking for anything.

**3** They had to use a _____ to try to find the expensive ring that was lost on the beach.

**4** Archaeologists have made an important _____ in Tutankhamen's tomb.

**5** By looking at artifacts from the past, we can learn a lot about people that _____ long ago.

**THINK BIG**

Pretend the year is 2500 AD. Make a list of three everyday objects that you want archaeologists to find and say why each object is important in your life.

_____

_____

_____

# Grammar

**19** Read and match. Write the letters.

___ **1** I need to get

___ **2** Have you ever had

___ **3** He needs to have

___ **4** They haven't had

___ **5** We are going to get

___ **6** Has she ever had

**a** her bicycle repaired?

**b** our hair cut.

**c** any of your poems published?

**d** my teeth checked.

**e** their letters posted yet.

**f** his laptop fixed.

**20** Complete the sentences. Use soon or yet.

**1** She'll get her computer repaired _____.

**2** He hasn't had his photograph taken _____.

**3** Are you going to get the car checked _____?

**4** Why haven't they returned their books _____?

**5** Alexa hasn't had her dress shortened _____.

**21** Unscramble and write.

**1** to get / fixed / we need / the roof

_____

**2** to have / when are / the jacket / you going / made

_____

**3** yet / he hasn't had / cut / the grass

_____

**4** their photos / where are / to have / taken / they going

_____

**5** shortened / to get / her skirt / she needs

_____

**6** his blood / how often / going to have / is he / tested

_____

**22** Make sentences using the phrases in the box. Use haven't had … yet or going to get … soon.

> mend button     test hearing     check homework
> repair laptop     stamp library book     change tire

**1** _____

**2** _____

**3** _____

**4** _____

**5** _____

**6** _____

**23** **Read and match. Write the letters.**

___ **1** antiquity

___ **2** compile

___ **3** honorary

___ **4** structure

___ **5** outstretched

___ **6** gladiator

**a** something built by people

**b** given to show respect or admiration to someone or something

**c** a man who fought other men and animals for entertainment in Ancient Rome

**d** to make a list using different pieces of information

**e** ancient times

**f** stretched out towards someone or something

**24** **Read and complete using the words in the box. Then listen and check.**

ancient    children    cultures    exist    hope

## The New Seven Wonders of the World

Do you know what the seven wonders of the world are? Over the years, there have been several different lists and many people around the world think they know what the wonders are, but they are not always correct. Although there are many amazing natural and man-made structures in our world, not all of them are one of the seven wonders. Let's read more about how today's list was compiled.

Over two thousand years ago in [1]_____ Greece, an engineer, Philon of Byzantium, created a list of the Seven Ancient Wonders of the World. Today, only one of those wonders of antiquity still exists: the pyramids of Egypt. In 1999, Bernard Weber, a Swiss adventurer, decided to create a new list of world wonders. He began the New 7 Wonders Foundation. This time, he wanted people from all around the world to choose the seven new wonders that [2]_____ today. He asked people to send in their votes for the new wonders. People voted by texting, voting online on the website, or calling in their votes. By 2007, more than 100 million people had voted. Who were these voters? Most of the voters were not adults. Bernard Weber is proud of the fact that they were mostly [3]_____ and young people.

Weber and a group of people reviewed all the votes. They chose the new seven wonders based on these criteria:

- The places should each have a unique beauty.
- The places should come from all over the world and represent people from all over the world.
- The places should be from different environments, such as deserts and rainforests.
- The places should be important to people from different [4]_____.
- The places should be located on different continents.

The final list of seven new wonders was decided. They are described on page 139 of your Student's Book. Weber was delighted by the enthusiasm and love that people showed for their cultures and other cultures. This enthusiasm and love, he believes, creates a feeling of [5]_____ for the future.

**25** Read 24 again and answer the questions.

**1** Which is the only remaining ancient wonder of the world?

_____

**2** Who began the New 7 Wonders Foundation?

_____

**3** Who voted for the new seven wonders?

_____

**4** How many criteria were used to choose the new seven wonders?

_____

**5** What does Weber say creates a feeling of hope for the future?

_____

**26** Complete the sentences using the words from 23.

**1** The Eiffel Tower in Paris is an amazing, man-made _____ .

**2** Spartacus was a famous Roman _____, who fought men and beasts in ancient times.

**3** You should _____ a list of all the places you'd like to visit in your lifetime.

**4** My aunt welcomed us with _____ arms when we arrived at her home after our long journey.

**5** Myths and legends about gods and goddesses have existed since _____.

**6** Although Eva was not a member of the History Society, she has been made an _____ one, because of all the research she has done on the local community.

**THINK BIG**

Pretend that you have to choose seven special places in your town or city. Which seven places are important to you, your family, and friends? Write about them and say why.

_____

_____

_____

_____

When you do research for a report, use an idea web to organize the information into categories. For example, if you write about a country, make categories for its location, population, and important cities.

When you write, make sure that you write only about one category of information in each paragraph.

**27** Look at the facts. Write the number of each fact in the correct category.

**1** between Pakistan and Burma

**2** Kolkata, Chennai, Bangalore, Mumbai

**3** southern Asia

**4** Hindi

**5** English—important language

**6** New Delhi—capital city

**7** one billion people

**8** seventh-largest country in the world

*The Republic of India*

*General Facts and Location*
_____
_____
_____

*Population, People and Languages*
_____
_____
_____

*Major Cities*
_____
_____
_____

**28** The paragraph below should only include general facts and information about the location of India. Circle the two sentences that do NOT belong in the paragraph.

The Republic of India is the seventh-largest country in the world. It's located in southern Asia. Hindi is its national language. It's situated between Pakistan and Burma. It's the seventh-largest country in the world. English is an important language, too.

**29** Write a report about India. Write three paragraphs. In paragraph 1, write about general facts and location. In paragraph 2, write about major cities. In paragraph 3, write about population, people, and languages. Use information in 27 and 28. Add information from your own research and your own idea web.

**THINK BIG**

What makes a country a good/bad place to live in? Why?

_____

_____

**30** Complete the sentences. Circle the letters.

1 A ___ is a place that's built for someone who has died.

   **a** tower            **b** mausoleum

2 The French gave the United States a ___ as a sign of friendship.

   **a** statue           **b** palace

3 There are famous ___ in both Egypt and Mexico.

   **a** mausoleums      **b** pyramids

**31** Complete the statements with the passive form of the verbs in the box.

> build      discover      locate      make

1 The Temple of Borobudur _____ by thousands of workers between 750 and 850 AD.

2 The Taj Mahal _____ in Agra, India.

3 The Taj Mahal _____ of white marble.

4 Victoria Falls _____ by David Livingstone in 1855.

**32** Combine the sentences. Use who and the sentences in the box.

> They helped to construct the Taj Mahal.
> They lived on Easter Island.

1 In Agra, India, there were more than 22,000 people.

_____

2 The Rapa Nui are Polynesian people.

_____

**33** Complete the sentences with the words in the box. Use get / have something done.

> cut         fixed         washed

1 My cell phone is broken. I need to _____.

2 Your hair is too long. You need to _____.

3 His jeans are dirty. He needs to _____.

# unit 9
# THAT'S ENTERTAINMENT!

**1** Read the statements. Circle the ones that describe you.

**1** Music is very important in my life.

**2** Reading is very important in my life.

**3** Video games are very important in my life.

**4** Movies are very important in my life.

**5** I like reading about singers and actors.

**6** I like animation more than regular movies.

**7** I like movies that scare me.

**8** I like talking about the concerts I go to.

**2** Read and circle.

|   |                                           | Sometimes | Often | Never |
|---|-------------------------------------------|-----------|-------|-------|
| **1** | I go to the movie theater.            | S         | O     | N     |
| **2** | I go to live concerts.                | S         | O     | N     |
| **3** | I go to bookstores or the library.    | S         | O     | N     |
| **4** | I go to festivals to see people perform. | S      | O     | N     |
| **5** | I watch movie award programs on TV.   | S         | O     | N     |
| **6** | I watch music contests on TV.         | S         | O     | N     |
| **7** | I read when I get bored.               | S         | O     | N     |
| **8** | I play video games when I get bored.  | S         | O     | N     |

**Complete the sentences. Use the words in the box.**

> book signing    comic book exhibition    concert
> festival        movie premiere           video game launch

1  People are walking around dressed up as Star Wars storm troopers, Avatar characters, and Mario. There are cool books, posters, T-shirts, and hats for sale. Going to a _____ is so much fun!

2  People are standing in line waiting until midnight to get into the store. Everybody wants to be the first to own the new game. This _____ is the best!

3  The place is full of people dancing and singing along with the performer on stage. The music is really loud! The tickets were expensive but worth it to see this singer in _____!

4  Photographers are taking pictures of the actors as they walk into the movie theater. People are so excited to see their favorite stars! Being at a _____ is incredible!

5  The author of the latest best-selling book is sitting behind a table. People are standing in line holding the book. A _____ is really fun to go to.

6  Thousands of people have come to see the dancers dressed in stunning traditional costumes dancing to folk music. People are in a wonderful mood for these two days at the _____.

 **THINK BIG**

If you went to a comic book exhibition and you could dress as any character, which character would you be? Why?

_____

_____

**4** Read and listen. Then read the statements and circle the correct names.

TV Programs
Movies
Music
Clothes
▼ Books
• Fiction
• Best Sellers
• Nonfiction
• Manga

## CUSTOMER REVIEWS

Bubble Sky!

5 stars: ★ ★ ★ ★ ★ 410 reviews

4 stars: ★★ ★★ ☆ 60 reviews
3 stars: ★ ★★ ☆☆ 12 reviews
2 stars: ★★ ☆☆☆ 0 reviews
1 star: ★ ☆☆☆☆ 1 review

### Display reviews by most helpful:

**Jennifer rated it** ★ ★★ ★★ I love manga but I don't usually read comedy manga. They seem so silly to me. Not *Bubble Sky*! The characters are hilarious and their adventures are like a puzzle—fun to work out. The main character, Seraphim Bubble, is always on the lookout for an adventure. Get this book! You won't regret it!

**Nicky rated it** ★ All my friends loved this book but I couldn't even finish it. Seraphim is boring. I don't like science much so I didn't find her solutions interesting. The only funny character is PunBun, Seraphim's pet bunny. The rest of the characters are dull. Period.

**Tim rated it** ★ ★★ ★ I agree with Jennifer that *Bubble Sky* is fun to read because of the characters. Another reviewer said that Seraphim was boring but I really think it's clever how Seraphim always gets everyone out of trouble using cool science ideas that no one else knows about. But I gave it four stars because sometimes the plot was predictable.

1 **Jennifer / Nicky / Tim** said that the characters were hilarious.

2 **Jennifer / Nicky / Tim** said that all her friends loved the book.

3 **Jennifer / Nicky / Tim** said that the plot was sometimes predictable.

 **5** Answer the questions.

1 Why did Jennifer like the adventures?

_____

2 Have you ever read manga? What would a manga book need to include for you to give it five stars?

_____

**6** Listen and read. Then answer the questions.

**Ann:** Mom? Um, could I possibly borrow fifteen dollars?

**Mom:** What for?

**Ann:** I want to go and see all the celebrities at the movie premiere of Spider-Man. All my friends are going. But I don't have enough money for the train.

**Mom:** What happened to your allowance?

**Ann:** I spent it on that concert last week. It was more expensive than I thought.

**Mom:** Well, I suppose I could give you next week's allowance in advance, but that means you won't get anything next week.

**Ann:** OK. Deal! Thanks, Mom.

**1** What does Ann want from her mom?

_____

**2** Ann won't get any allowance money next week. Why?

_____

**7** Look at 6. Circle the correct answers.

**1** When Mom says "What for?" she means ___.

   **a** Why do you need it?     **b** What do you mean?

**2** "In advance" means ___.

   **a** an increase     **b** early

**3** When Ann says "Deal!" she means ___.

   **a** I agree.     **b** Let's play cards.

**8** Complete the dialog with the underlined expressions in 6. Listen and check your answers.

**John:** Do you want to stop at the shopping mall on the way home?

**Jim:** ¹_____

**John:** I need some things for my science project.

**Jim:** OK. But only if we go to the pizza place in there first. I'm so hungry!

**John:** OK. ²_____

| Direct speech | Reported speech |
|---|---|
| Claire said, "The album **isn't** as good as the last one." | Claire said (that) the album **wasn't** as good as the last one. |
| Josh said, "**I'm going** to the premiere." | Josh said (that) he **was going** to the premiere. |

**9** Read the dialogs and answer the questions. Use reported speech.

**Katie:** Hey, Joe! What are you doing tonight?

**Joe:** I'm going to a live concert at Dragon's Den to see One Direction. What about you?

**Katie:** I'm not doing anything.

**1** What's Joe doing tonight?

_____

**2** What's Katie doing tonight?

_____

**Sam:** The new *Play to Win 2* video game is really challenging.

**Joanne:** It's much better than *Play to Win 1*.

**3** What did Sam say about *Play to Win 2*?

_____

**4** What did Joanne say about *Play to Win 2*?

_____

**Nina:** I want to go to the comic book exhibition!

**John:** Me, too! I'm going to dress up as Mario.

**5** Where did Nina want to go?

_____

**6** What did John say?

_____

**10** Read the dialog and complete the sentences. Use reported speech.

I don't want to miss the book signing at the bookstore today. My mom's taking me.

I'm very excited. I'm going with my friend to a video game launch today!

1 He _____ he _____ to miss the book signing.

2 He _____ his mom _____ him.

3 She _____ she _____ very excited.

4 She _____ she _____ to a video game launch.

**11** Read the dialog and answer the questions. Use reported speech.

**Janet:** Hi, Charles. Where are you going?

**Charles:** I'm going to the movie theater with a friend.

**Janet:** You're lucky. My friend doesn't want to go with me. I don't want to go by myself. But I really want to see the new *Bubble Sky* movie.

**Charles:** Come with us.

**Janet:** Seriously? Thanks!

1 What did Charles say about his plans?

_____

2 What did Janet say about her friend?

_____

3 What did she say about going to the movie theater by herself?

_____

4 What did she say she wanted to do?

_____

**12** Match the words with the definitions. Write the letters.

|        |   |           |   |                                                                     |
|--------|---|-----------|---|---------------------------------------------------------------------|
| ____ | **1** | arcade    | **a** | to try to win at something                                      |
| ____ | **2** | compete   | **b** | pictures or images                                              |
| ____ | **3** | graphics  | **c** | the number of points a player gets in a game                   |
| ____ | **4** | score     | **d** | a flat surface that contains the controls for a machine        |
| ____ | **5** | industry  | **e** | a small machine or tool used for a specific purpose            |
| ____ | **6** | device    | **f** | all the businesses that work in a particular type of trade or service |
| ____ | **7** | console   | **g** | a special room or building where people go to play video games |

148

**13** Listen and read. Why are today's video games better?

## Video Games: The Year 2000 and Now

Have you ever asked your parents which computer and video games they played when they were younger? Perhaps they played Pac-Man® or Donkey Kong®? Maybe they had a Game Boy® at home and enjoyed playing Tetris® on it? The changes to the computer and video games industry since your parents were young have been incredible. Even since the year 2000, new technology has changed how, where, and what people play, as well as who they play with. We have many more choices now than we used to.

### How People Play and Who They Play With

In the year 2000, people played on game consoles, desktop computers, or in arcades. When they wanted to play with others, they invited them over to their houses, or they played alone. Some online games were available at the end of the 1990s, but they were expensive and not as many people had access to the Internet. Today, people can play games anywhere they want on portable gaming devices, phones, or tablets. They can play online with friends or even with other players from around the world.

### What People Play

Games today have graphics that are sharper and more lifelike than they used to be, and new technology has made games more challenging, with more variety. Since 2000, Massively Multi-player Online games (MMOs) have become popular. People like to compete against each other for higher scores. They love virtual worlds that offer experiences they could never have in real life. Dancing and exercise games, as well as sports and adventure games, have also become popular.

This trend towards more choices and deeper involvement in virtual worlds will continue to change video games well into the future. Who knows what video games will be available when you are an adult! The children of the future will probably think that the games you play today are very old-fashioned!

**14** Read **13** again and answer the questions.

**1**  How has new technology changed video games since the year 2000?

_____

**2**  Why did few people play online games before the year 2000?

_____

**3**  How are today's games different from those in the past?

_____

**4**  Why do people like MMO games?

_____

**15** Complete the sentences using the words from **12**.

**1**  My brother loves to_____ against others in different sports.

**2**  Our father has a very useful _____ for lighting fires when we are camping.

**3**  I really like the _____ in that game, because they seem so real!

**4**  Uncle Zac said that he used to spend a lot of time playing video games at an _____ when he was young.

**5**  The computer games _____ has developed a great deal in the past 15 years.

**6**  Each time they play, they try to improve their _____ and win the game.

**7**  The first video game _____ was a large box with two attached controllers.

**THINK BIG**

Some people feel that video games are bad for young people. Do you agree or disagree? Why?

_____

_____

# Grammar

**16** **Read and match.**

1 Francesca asked me to
2 The head teacher told us
3 Samuel's parents told him
4 The traffic officer told the driver
5 The librarian asked the children
6 Grandma asked us

a to pull over and show his driver's licence.
b to return their books before the holidays.
c bring my favorite food to the party.
d not to make too much noise, because she was feeling sick.
e to tell our families about the school fair.
f to write a letter of apology to his music teacher.

**17** **Complete the sentences using the words in the box.**

> asked    feed    his    to    told    us

1 We _____ our mother to give us a lift to the concert.
2 His grandfather _____ him to try harder on the soccer field .
3 Leyla asked her cousin to _____ the fish while she was away.
4 He told Mehmet _____ return his DVD game later.
5 Our art teacher asked _____ not to leave the paintbrushes dirty.
6 His mother told him to clean up _____ bedroom.

**18** **Unscramble and write the sentences.**

1 her sister / a game / Efe asked / to play

_____

2 our pajamas / told us / my aunt / to bring

_____

3 bake cookies / to help / asked me / Grandma

_____

4 to move away / the firefighter / from the building / told everyone

_____

**19** Write the sentences in reported speech. Use He / She told or He / She asked.

Mom, please help me.

1 _____

Deniz, don't do that!

2 _____

Look, everyone!

3 _____

Please take it, Dad.

4 _____

**20** Read and complete the sentences for you. Then write it in reported speech. Use I told...
or I asked... .

It is cold in the classroom.　　Please _____ .

1 _____

Your brother is annoying you.　　Don't _____ .

2 _____

You need help with your work.　　Please _____ .

3 _____

Your friend is late.　　You _____ .

4 _____

**21** Read and match. Write the letters.

| | | | | |
|---|---|---|---|---|
| ___ | **1** associate | | **a** | a long piece of music |
| ___ | **2** distinctive | | **b** | to make or think of something completely new |
| ___ | **3** carve | | **c** | very different from other things and easy to recognize |
| ___ | **4** invent | | **d** | complicated or difficult |
| ___ | **5** complex | | **e** | to make a connection between two things in your mind |
| ___ | **6** composition | | **f** | to cut a piece of wood or stone |

**22** Read and complete using the words in the box. Then listen and check.

> concerts    flutes    plastic    sounds    unusual

# Unique Musical Instruments

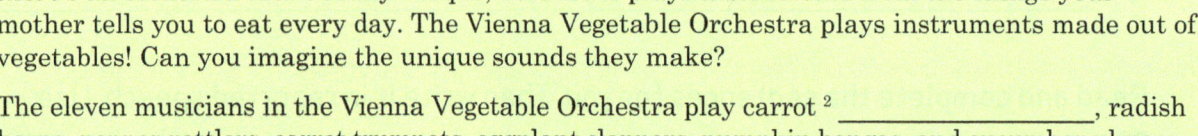

Every culture has musical instruments that are unique to it. The instruments are often made from a variety of materials such as wood, steel, animal bones, and ¹ _____. Many people are proud of the musical instruments that are associated with their cultures. Often these instruments make distinctive sounds, too–like no other sound that you've heard before. In Vienna, there's an orchestra that's really unique, because it plays instruments from the things your mother tells you to eat every day. The Vienna Vegetable Orchestra plays instruments made out of vegetables! Can you imagine the unique sounds they make?

The eleven musicians in the Vienna Vegetable Orchestra play carrot ² _____, radish horns, pepper rattlers, carrot trumpets, eggplant clappers, pumpkin bongos, and cucumber phones. The orchestra plays contemporary, jazz, and electronic music, among other styles. They play ³ _____ around the world. At the end of their concerts, the members of the audience receive a bowl of vegetable soup to enjoy. So, not only do you get to hear ⁴ _____ music, but you get to taste something delicious, too! The third album of the Vienna Vegetable Orchestra is called *Onionoise* and includes songs entitled "Nightshades" and "Transplants." Can you think of any other suitable titles for their compositions?

Why did this group of visual artists, poets, designers, and writers choose vegetables to create music? They were fascinated by the challenge to produce musical ⁵ _____ using natural foods. They constantly experiment with vegetables to create new and complex sounds. As part of their work, they give workshops on how to create instruments from vegetables. A morning TV program said it was, "…a highly unusual, tasty performance."

You knew vegetables were good for you. Now you know that they sound good, too! What's your favorite vegetable? Can you think of a musical instrument that you could make out of it?

**23** Read 22 again and choose the correct answers.

1 Musical instruments are often made out of materials like plastic, steel, wood, and
_____.

    **a** animal feathers         **b** animal bones

2 The Vienna Vegetable Orchestra plays electronic, jazz, and _____.

    **a** contemporary music         **b** classical music

3 At the end of a concert, a bowl of soup is given to the _____.

    **a** audience         **b** orchestra

4 The orchestra teaches people how to _____.

    **a** make soup from vegetables         **b** make instruments from vegetables

**24** Complete the sentences using the words in the box.

> audience     constantly     eggplants     contemporary
> unique     radishes     performance

1 The orchestra gave a wonderful _____ of Mozart's Symphony Number 2.

2 The sitar makes a _____ sound, which is associated with Indian classical music.

3 Some people like _____ music, which is modern, while others like traditional music.

4 The _____ loved the Vienna Vegetable Orchestra's concert, especially when they got soup afterwards!

5 The musicians are _____ trying out new sounds with their unusual instruments.

6 _____ are long and purple; _____ are small and red.

**THINK BIG**

Review the vegetable instruments used by the Vienna Vegetable Orchestra in 22 again. Think of three other vegetables that the Vienna Vegetable Orchestra could use to make instruments. Say why.

_____

_____

A good movie review briefly describes the important parts of the movie: the story, the hero and characters, and your opinion (what you liked and didn't like).

Before you write, make a chart that includes these topics and add vivid adjectives such as *stunning*, *captivating*, *tense*, *dull*, and *boring*.

When you write, order your ideas. Write about the story first but don't give away the ending! Some people want the ending to be a surprise. Then write about the characters. Describe them and what they do. Finally, describe what you liked and didn't like (for example, the acting or special effects).

**25** Put the paragraphs in order. Write 1, 2, or 3.

## Review of *Bubble Sky: the Movie*

____ Some of the acting is fabulous! Melinda Mendez is very good as Seraphim Bubble. Brad Davis is hilarious as Tran. The evil Ms. Doze, played by Vivian Bell, is captivating but Sandy Dennis as the teacher is dull. The special effects are stunning! All in all, this was a very cool film!

____ *Bubble Sky* is a captivating animation adventure. In the story, a young girl discovers that her school is taken over by aliens. She figures out that a particular herb might destroy them. She needs to find the herb and then get the aliens to eat it.

____ Seraphim Bubble is the hero of the story. Her pet rabbit, PunBun, gives good advice. Seraphim's younger brother Tran and her friend Gayle help her fight the aliens.

**26** Look at 25. Complete the chart about *Bubble Sky*.

| The story | The hero and characters | The opinion (what you liked and didn't like) |
|---|---|---|
|  |  |  |

**27** Write a review of a movie playing near you this weekend. Make a chart to help you.

**28** Circle the correct events.

1 The author arrived late for the **movie premiere** / **book signing**. The manager of the bookstore was upset because people were waiting.

2 My brother and I went to the **comic book exhibition** / **video game launch**. We dressed up as Mario and Pikachu. There were thousands of people there.

3 My town is having an arts and crafts **concert** / **festival**. For three days, painters, potters, and jewelry makers will be selling their work.

4 This Friday night, all the stars will be at the **movie premiere** / **festival** of the new Superman movie.

5 The **concert** / **launch** tickets for The Eyes go on sale next Tuesday. They'll sell out fast!

**29** Read and correct the one mistake in each reported speech sentence.

1 **Carol:** I'm tired.

**Reported speech:** She says she was tired.

_____

2 **Jason:** I'm going to be at the launch tomorrow.

**Reported speech:** He said he is going to be at the launch tomorrow.

_____

3 **Diana:** I want to meet the author of the book.

**Reported speech:** She said she want to meet the author of the book.

_____

4 **Will:** I don't like sci-fi movies.

**Reported speech:** He said he doesn't like sci-fi movies.

_____

**30** Write the sentences using reported speech. Use asked or told.

1 **Lara:** Listen to the song, Daphne.

_____

2 **Paul:** Mom, don't go to the festival.

_____

**THINK BIG**

**I** Look at the pictures. Complete the items. Add your own items on the extra lines.

## MYSTERIOUS EVENTS

**1** Northern _____

**2** _____ circles

**3** Bermuda _____

**4** _____

## FAMOUS PLACES

**1** _____ of Borobudur

**2** _____ of Liberty

**3** _____ of Kukulcán

**4** _____

## SPECIAL EVENTS

**1** _____ signing

**2** rock _____

**3** movie _____

**4** _____

**2** Find a famous place or event that interests you. Complete the chart.

| Name of the place or event | _____ |
|---|---|
| When was it built, discovered, or found?<br>When did it take place? Where is it located? | _____<br>_____ |
| Is this a place or event that was mentioned in a song?<br>What's the name of the song?<br>Who's the singer?<br>What are the lines (the lyrics) that mention the place? | _____<br>_____<br>_____<br>_____ |
| This place or event was described in a book, online, or in a magazine, wasn't it?<br>What was the title of the book or article?<br>What did the writer say about it? | _____<br>_____<br>_____ |

**3** Do research. Find more information about the place or event in **2** that interests you. Write a report about the place or event.

_____

_____

_____

_____

_____

_____

_____

_____

_____

_____

**1** Read Julia's plan for her science report. Write questions and answers.
Use yet and already.

### The Importance of the Monarch Butterfly
by Julia Black

| Monday | Tuesday | Wednesday | Thursday | Friday |
|---|---|---|---|---|
| Morning: Go to Museum of Natural History, draw Monarch butterflies. Afternoon: Write questions about the butterflies. | Morning: Do research on Monarch butterflies and answer my questions. | Morning: Write my report on Monarch butterflies. | Morning: Create my presentation. | Morning: Hand in my report and give presentation. |

**1**  It's Monday afternoon.

**Q:** (Julia / go to the museum) _____

**A:** _____

**2**  It's Tuesday.

**Q:** (write / her report) _____

**A:** _____

**3**  It's Tuesday afternoon.

**Q:** (she / do her research) _____

**A:** _____

**4**  It's Thursday afternoon.

**Q:** (she / create her presentation) _____

**A:** _____

**5**  It's Thursday afternoon.

**Q:** (she / give her presentation) _____

**A:** _____

**1** Complete the sentences with the present perfect progressive form of the verbs and
for or since.

**1** Jimmy Woodard _____ (take)
computers apart _____ he was five years old.

**2** Caitlyn _____ (play) chess
_____ she was very young.

**3** Serena _____ (study) martial
arts _____ five years.

**4** I _____ (collect) stamps _____ two years.

**2** Ask and answer questions about the chart. Use the present perfect and for or since.

| Mr. Freedman's Class – Hobbies | | |
|---|---|---|
| **Student** | **Hobby** | **How Long?** |
| Rob | collects coins | four years |
| Cynthia | makes jewelry | she was nine |
| David | draws cartoon characters | three years |
| Iris | has dance lessons | six months |

**1** How long _____
_____

**2** How long _____
_____

**3** _____
_____

**4** _____
_____

**1** **Complete the sentences with the correct form of the verb in parenthesis.**

*How will you help your family and friends?*

**1** If I _____ (finish) my homework early, I'll help with the chores.

**2** If my sister doesn't understand her homework, I _____ (help) her.

**3** I _____ (call) my friend if he's sick.

**4** If my dad _____ (ask) me to walk the dog, I _____ (do) it.

**5** I _____ (tell) my parents if I _____ (break) something.

**2** **Complete the sentences.**

**1** If someone gives me a present, _____.

**2** If someone in my family is sick, _____.

**3** If my friend gets upset with me, _____.

**4** If I don't feel well, _____.

**3** **Read and match. Write the letter.**

*Advice to a New Exchange Student at School*

___ **1** You're new.

___ **2** Some people are mean to you.

___ **3** You don't speak the language well.

___ **4** You're always late for lessons.

**a** Get organized so that you get to lessons on time.

**b** Don't worry about your mistakes. Speak anyway.

**c** Join clubs so that you meet people.

**d** Stay away from those people.

**4** **Write the sentences in 3 with should or shouldn't.**

**1** _____

**2** _____

**3** _____

**4** _____

**5** **Complete the sentences.**

**1** _____, you should ask them to stop.

**2** _____, you should apologize.

**3** _____, you should get help.

**1** Read. Then circle the best answers.

|  | I like | I don't like |
|---|---|---|
| **Emily** | languages<br>writing and blogging<br>big families<br>living close to family | sports |
| **Al** | making money<br>all sports<br>studying hard<br>living in other countries | languages |

1  In 10 years, **Emily / Al** will definitely be studying languages at college.

2  In 10 years, **Emily / Al** probably will be running and hiking at the weekends.

3  In 10 years, **Emily / Al** probably won't be living in the same city.

4  In 20 years, **Emily / Al** will definitely be running an international business.

5  In 20 years, **Emily / Al** probably will be writing books.

**2** Read. Then complete the sentences with I'll be or I won't be and the words in parenthesis.

*What will you be doing in 20 years?*

1  Celia: I love animals. I don't like living in the city. I like traveling.

   a  _____ (work as a vet)

   b  _____ (live in the country)

   c  _____ (go on vacation to the same place every year)

2  Jeff: I love biology and helping people. I don't like cooking. I like boats.

   a  _____ (finish medical school)

   b  _____ (work as a chef)

   c  _____ (sail my boat)

**3** Answer the questions about yourself. Use No, definitely not, Yes, definitely, Probably not or Yes, probably.

1  In seven years will you be at college? _____

2  In two years will you be blogging? _____

3  Next year will you be in Middle School? _____

**1** Complete the dialogs. Use the phrases in the box.

> join some clubs                          start a blog
> start reading fun things like manga comics    have lots of singing lessons

1 **Rita:** I want to be a singer when I grow up.

   **Eddie:** If I were you, _____.

2 **John:** I don't enjoy reading.

   **Nancy:** If I were you, _____.

3 **Tom:** I'm bored all the time.

   **Kristy:** If I were you, _____.

4 **Grace:** I like writing a lot.

   **Sam:** If I were you, _____.

**2** Complete the sentences. Circle the correct verbs.

1 If you **will get / got** up earlier, you **wouldn't be / won't be** late for school all the time.

2 If the world **could have / can have** superheroes, it **would be / was** a safer place to live.

3 If he **practiced / will practice** the guitar more, he **will play / would play** better.

4 If our chess team **will win / won** more matches, we **will compete / would compete** in the national championships.

**3** Unscramble the phrases. Complete and answer the questions.

1 (live / could / you / if / anywhere)

   _____,

   where would you live?

   I _____.

2 (you / choose / which / would)
   If you could choose your own super powers,

   _____?

   I _____.

3 (didn't / if / have / computers / we)

   _____,

   what would we do?

   We _____.

**1** Complete the sentences. Circle the correct words.

1 Pandas only live in China. Brown bears live in many countries. Pandas live in **more / fewer** places than brown bears.

2 Brown bears spend **less / more** time eating than pandas. Pandas need to eat lots of bamboo every day to get enough nutrients.

3 Parakeets have **fewer / more** legs than dogs.

4 Parakeets eat **more / less** food than dogs.

**2** Read the facts. Then complete the sentences using most, least or fewest and the words in parenthesis.

> **Facts**
> Monserrat has <u>less</u> crime than other countries.
> Greater London has <u>more</u> people than other counties in England.
> North America has <u>more</u> meat-eating plants than any other continent.
> Canada has very <u>few</u> species of mammals. It has fewer than any other country.
> People in Papua, New Guinea, speak <u>more</u> languages than people in other countries.
> Taki Taki, the language of Suriname, has <u>few</u> words.

1 Greater London has the _____ of any other county in England. (people)

2 People in Papua, New Guinea, speak the _____ of any country. (languages)

3 Canada has _____ of any country. (species of mammals)

4 North America has the _____ of any continent. (meat-eating plants)

5 The language of Taki Taki has the _____ of all languages. (words)

6 The country of Monserrat has the _____ of all countries. (crime)

**3** Write sentences with the words in the box. Use superlatives.

1 The sun bear lives in Southeast Asia. It is only 1.2 meters tall. It is _____ in the world.

2 No bird is taller than the ostrich. The ostrich is _____ in the world.

3 No animal on land is larger than the elephant. The elephant is _____ on land.

4 No animal is louder than the blue whale. The blue whale is _____ in the world.

> large / creature
> loud / animal
> small / bear
> tall / bird

**1** **Complete the sentences. Write the correct words.**

1 Kryptos is a sculpture in the United States, _____ it?

   is       isn't

2 The fourth section of Kryptos isn't solved, _____ it?

   is       isn't

3 There are many people trying to solve it, _____ there?

   are      aren't

4 Code breakers can't solve it, _____ they?

   can      can't

5 Anyone can try to crack the code, _____ they?

   can      can't

**2** **Write question tags to complete the questions.**

1 The Great Pyramids of Egypt are beautiful, _____?

2 The Sailing Stones aren't a mystery any more, _____?

3 The Bermuda Triangle is mysterious, _____?

4 You can climb the pyramids in Mexico, _____?

**3** **Unscramble the sentences and add words to make question tags.**

1 found out / scientists / in the early 20th century / about the Nazca Lines

_____

2 the Nazcans created / the lines / don't / scientists / know why

_____

3 drew / the Nazcans / animal and plant figures

_____

4 the lines / need to see / you / from a plane

_____

5 didn't know / you / about the Nazca Lines

_____

**1** Complete the sentences. Circle the correct verbs.

**1** The Mona Lisa **paints** / **was painted** by Leonardo da Vinci.

**2** The Taj Mahal **was built** / **built** by the emperor of India.

**3** The Church of San Francisco de Asis in New Mexico **damaged** / **was damaged** by an earthquake in 1906.

**4** The Statue of Liberty and the Eiffel Tower **were designed** / **designed** by the same French designer.

**2** Write these sentences in the passive.

**1** The people of Egypt built the Great Pyramids of Egypt.

_____

**2** Someone moved the Moai statues of Easter Island.

_____

**3** Write sentences in the passive. Use the verbs in the box.

> carve     destroy     name     trade

**1** The city of Petra, Jordan / one of the seven wonders of the world in 2007

_____

**2** The city of Petra / out of the sandstone mountains in the Jordan desert

_____

_____

**3** Spices, perfumes and other things / in Petra

_____

_____

**4** The city of Petra / by an earthquake in 363 AD / nearly

_____

_____

**4** Complete the sentences with the names of places in your country.

**1** _____ is visited every year by thousands of tourists.

**2** _____ is known as one of the most beautiful places in my country.

**3** _____ is said to be one of the most mysterious places in my country.

**1** **What did the people say about the movie?**
**Change the sentences to reported speech.**

| Claire: | The acting is incredible. |
|---|---|
| Jeff: | The music is really cool. |
| Mira: | It isn't the director's best film. |
| Nancy: | It's definitely going to win an Oscar. |
| Tom: | It's not that entertaining. |

**1** Claire _____.

**2** Jeff _____.

**3** Mira _____.

**4** Nancy _____.

**5** Tom _____.

**2** **Change the sentences to reported speech.**

**Tina:** I'm going to a Justin Bieber concert for my birthday.

**Paul:** I'm going to a movie premiere to see Jennifer Lawrence.

**1** Tina _____.

**2** Paul _____.

**Mike:** I want to buy the new *Cats* video game.

**Sheila:** I don't like playing video games.

**3** Mike _____.

**4** Sheila _____.

**Tonya:** I'm not going to the book signing.

**Freddie:** I always go to book signings.

**5** She _____.

**6** He _____.

# Young Learners English Practice
# Flyers

Note to students:
These practice materials will help you prepare
for the YLE (Young Learners English) Tests.
There are three kinds of practice materials in this
sampler:
Listening, Reading & Writing and Speaking.
Good luck!

# Young Learner's English Practice Flyers: Listening A

## – 5 questions –

 Listen and draw lines. There is one example.

Bella          David          Harry          Katy

Richard          Robert          Sarah

**– 5 questions –**

 **Listen and write. There is one example.**

Interview with a Star

**Career:** _soccer player_

1 | **How many years:** _____ years

2 | **When playing in Olympics:** in _____ months

3 | **Olympic goal:** _____ medal

4 | **Plans in ten years:** _____

5 | **Message for young people:** _____

**– 5 questions –**

 **Listen and check (✔) the box. There is one example.**

What time does the concert start?

A ☐

B ✓

C ☐

1  What subject did Mary choose for her history project?

A ☐

B ☐

C ☐

2  What did Tom buy?

A ☐

B ☐

C ☐

3   Which country would Bill like to visit?

**A** ☐

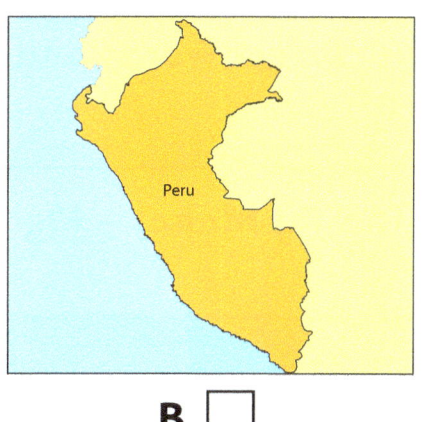

**B** ☐

**C** ☐

4   What homework is Katy going to do tonight?

$$a + b = c$$
$$a - b = d$$

**A** ☐

**B** ☐

**C** ☐

5   Which structure is Emma learning about?

**A** ☐

**B** ☐

**C** ☐

**– 8 questions –**

**Read the text. Choose the correct words and write them on the lines.**

---

### The Taj Mahal – My Dream Trip!

**Example**

If I ___could___ visit anywhere in the world, I would love to visit the Taj Mahal in India. The Taj Mahal is a gigantic

1   mausoleum that _____ by the emperor Shah Jahan

2   in memory of his wife. It _____ near the city of Agra. I think it has to be the most stunning monument _____

3   can be found in India.

4   There are more _____ two million people who visit

5   the Taj Mahal every year. It gets _____ visitors than Buckingham Palace in London.

6   My uncle visited the Taj Mahal last year and he _____ the weather was amazing and it was really beautiful. I

7   haven't saved enough money for my trip _____

8   but I can't wait to go someday. If I could, I _____ go tomorrow!

---

| **Example** | can | will | could |
|---|---|---|---|
| 1 | build | is building | was built |
| 2 | located | is located | was located |
| 3 | that | who | when |
| 4 | of | to | than |
| 5 | more | most | the most |
| 6 | said | tell | say |
| 7 | now | already | yet |
| 8 | do | would | will |

## – 5 questions –

**Richard is talking to his friend, Harry. What does Harry say?**

**Read the conversation and choose the best answer. Write a letter (A–H) for each answer.**

**You do not need to use all the letters.**

**Example**

**Richard:** What are you doing this weekend?

**Harry:** ___B___.

## Questions

1    **Richard:**  What's your report about?

     **Harry:**  _____

2    **Richard:**  That's hard to write about, isn't it?

     **Harry:**  _____

3    **Richard:**  I don't have any homework. I'm going to a soccer match on Sunday afternoon.

     **Harry:**  _____

4    **Richard:**  Maybe you can. Have you started your report yet?

     **Harry:**  _____

5    **Richard:**  Well, get busy. If you finish the report early, you can come with us.

     **Harry:**  _____

A  Good idea. I'll get started now.

B  I have to finish a report by Monday. **(Example)**

C  I don't think it's hard. It's interesting.

D  I don't, do you?

E  It's about life in the future.

F  No, I haven't.

G  If I were you, I'd get started straight away.

H  I wish I could go with you.

## – 7 questions –

**Look at the picture and read the story. Write some words to complete the sentences about the story. You can use 1, 2, 3 or 4 words.**

### A Discovery in the Back Garden

My name's Robert and I have an amazing story to tell. Most people don't believe me when I tell them about it but it's completely true.

One day, my friend Sarah brought a small potted tree to my house. My mom said it was OK for us to plant the tree in the back garden. While I was digging, I found something hard and round.

"What is it?" Sarah asked.

"I'm not sure," I said, "but I think it's a coin."

We brushed it off and looked at it more closely. It wasn't perfectly round and it wasn't very shiny but it was definitely a coin or a token of some kind. On one side was a picture of a man's face. He had a big nose and looked very serious. The word "Roma" was printed on the other side.

Sarah thought it might be a bus token from Italy. We decided to take it to the museum. An expert looked at the coin. She said it was from ancient Rome. "You've discovered an important piece of history," she said.

"This is very mysterious," I said. "I wonder how it got into my back garden?"

Like I said, most people don't believe me when I tell this story. If you don't believe me, you can go to the museum and see the coin for yourself.

## Examples

The person telling this story is called _____Robert_____.

Most people _____don't believe_____ him when he tells this story.

## Questions

1  One day, Sarah brought a small _____ to Robert's house.

2  Robert's mom said it was OK to _____ in the back garden.

3  Robert found something that was _____ and round while he was digging.

4  On one side of the coin, there was a picture of _____.

5  On the other side of the coin, the word "Roma" _____.

6  Robert went to _____ and spoke to an expert.

7  The expert said the discovery was an important _____.

Find the differences

**Candidate's copy**

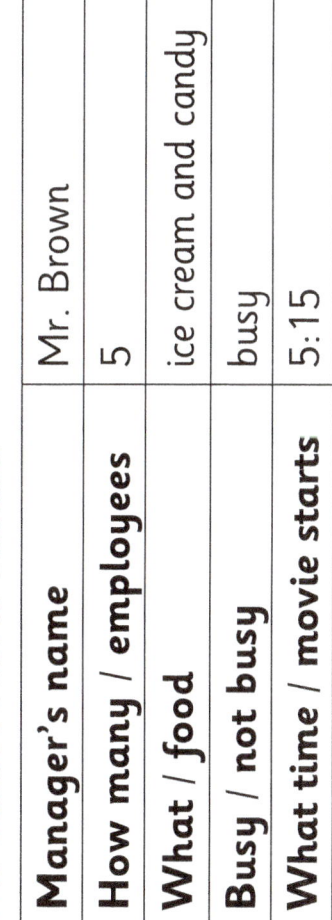

### The Vine Movie Theater

| Manager's name | ? |
|---|---|
| How many / employees | ? |
| What / food | ? |
| Busy / not busy | ? |
| What time / movie starts | ? |

**Information exchange**

### The Sunset Movie Theater

| Manager's name | Mr. Brown |
|---|---|
| How many / employees | 5 |
| What / food | ice cream and candy |
| Busy / not busy | busy |
| What time / movie starts | 5:15 |

**Student B**

I need to buy some glue so I can finish my model.

I've been learning about the solar system in school and I like it.

Yes, I want to do a project about Pablo Picasso.

I need to write a report about him and make a big poster to show some of his works of art.

Yes, I want to do a project about the solar system.

Yes, I've written my report but I haven't built the model yet.

No, I haven't. I'm going to start looking at some websites about him on the Internet.

I need to build a model of the solar system and write a report about it.

Yes, I need to buy some ink for our printer. I need to print out some of his paintings.

I've been learning about him in art and I like his paintings.

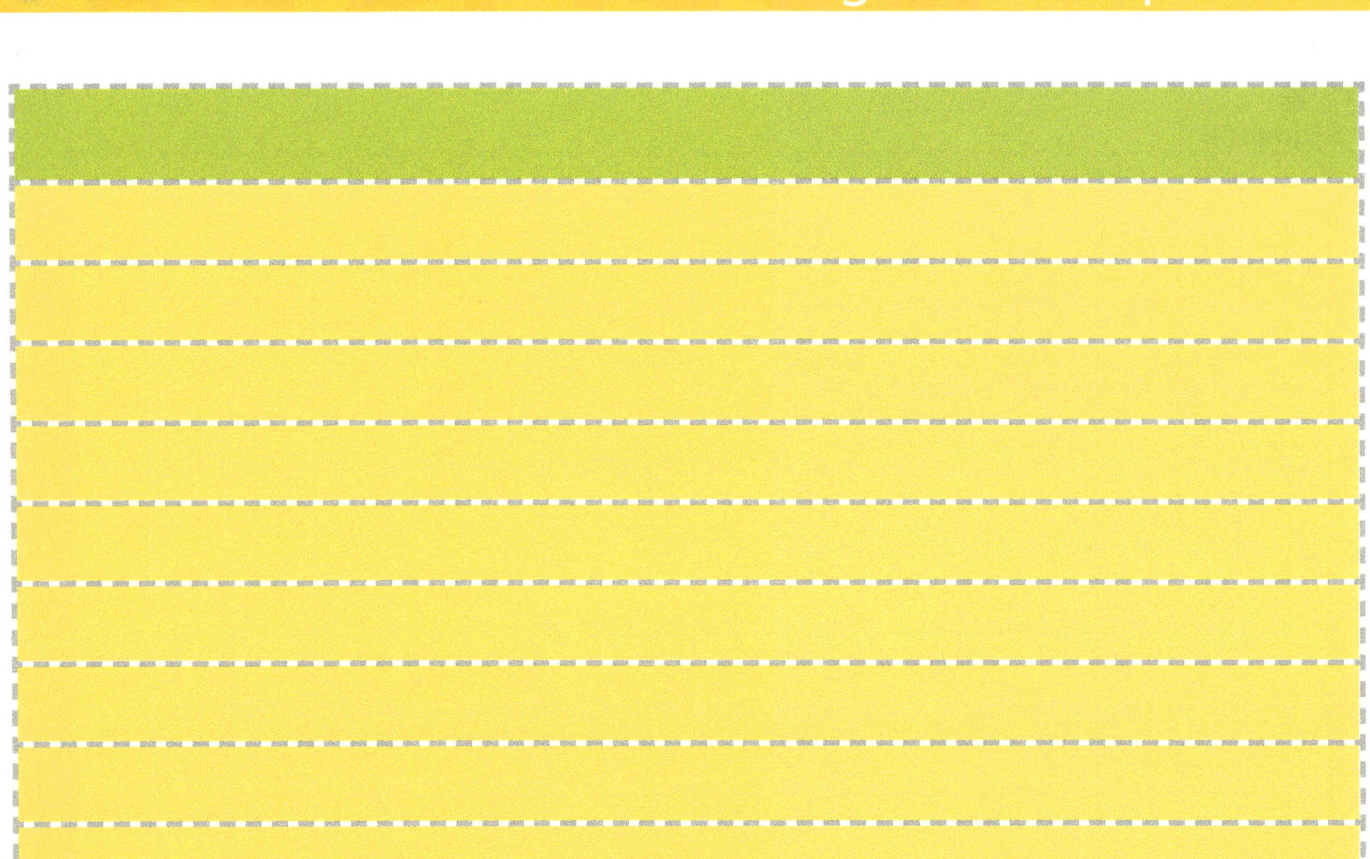

**Mystery Classmate:** _____

(Remember: Don't read the name aloud!)

??? 

If this person could eat any food every day, it would be

_____.

He/She plays more _____ than _____.

He/She reads fewer _____ than _____.

He/She definitely spends _____ time in front of the
computer than some people I know.

If he/she didn't have to go to school every day, he/she would

_____ and _____ from morning till night.

My classmate thinks he/she will probably be living in _____
in twenty years. And he'll/she'll probably be working as a(n)

_____.

Who is he/she?

**Description cards**

One set for the group leader

One set for each group

**International Mystery Solvers**

It's a new video game about explorers…

…who are trying to solve the mystery of a lost island civilization.

**Chasing Bigfoot**

It's a new comic book about a team of explorers…

…who travel by boat and plane into a danger zone in search of answers.

**Return to Atlantis**

It's a new movie about a group of scientists…

…who are looking for a giant, mysterious creature that lives in the forests of North America.

**Inside the Bermuda Triangle**

It's a new sci-fi book about some scientists…

…who go from country to country searching for answers to the world's most hard-to-solve mysteries.

**Review cards**

One set for each group member

Your best friend says, "It's amazing!"

Your best friend says, "It's interesting."

Your best friend says, "It's quite boring."

Your best friend says, "It's awful."